D1552782

It All Started with Stones and Clubs

It All Started with

STONES

AND

CLUBS

BEING A *Short History* OF *War*
AND *Weaponry* FROM *Earliest Times*
TO THE *Present,* NOTING THE
Gratifying Progress MADE BY *Man*
SINCE HIS *First Crude, Small-
Scale Efforts* TO *Do Away* WITH *Those
Who Disagreed* WITH HIM.

By RICHARD ARMOUR

McGRAW-HILL BOOK COMPANY

NEW YORK   TORONTO   LONDON   SYDNEY

ACKNOWLEDGMENT

I am indebted to Chairman Mao Tse-tung for his inspiring statement: "War is the highest form of struggle for resolving contradictions."

R. A.

CONTENTS

It All Started with Stones and Clubs

CHAPTER I

Primitive Man

BACK in the Stone Age, man was too uncivilized and unimaginative to wage war. All he did was eat and sleep and try to keep warm. He also reproduced, though he did not know this was what he was doing when he did it.

Stone Age man was very little above the animal.[1] Fortunately for his status, animals did not wage war either, so man did not develop an inferiority complex. Unlike man, animals never progressed to the point of making war. This is one reason why animals have remained animals and, over the centuries, have lagged so far behind man.

Not only was man too uncivilized to wage war during the Stone Age, but he had no reason to do so.

He had no desire to take territory away from other

[1] In fact when animals were in trees, he was below the animal, which made him uneasy.

men, since he had more territory (and more stones) than he could possibly use.

He had no desire to take *anything* away from anybody else, because every man had roughly the same things: a rough, cold cave, a rough, cold wife, and an empty stomach.

He did not declare war when someone came bounding over his boundary, because there were no boundaries. There were not even any walls or barbed wire or border guards or customs officials.

He did not declare war out of dislike for someone else's ideology, because everyone had the same ideology, which was: Try To Stay Alive If You Can.

He did not wage war to save national honor, because there were no nations and there was no honor. Nor did he wage war to save face, face at that time being only the front part of the head and in no danger of being lost unless the whole head was.

He was not stimulated to declare war by reading books or newspapers or hearing over the radio or TV about what people on the other side were planning to do to him if he didn't do it to them first.

In fact there was no other side. This shows how primitive primitive man was.

Had man remained in this unhappy condition, there would have been no fortunes made through the manufacture of munitions, no memoirs ghostwritten for generals, no heroes, no medals, no war orphans, no national cemeteries. There would be no veterans' benefits, no veterans' hospitals. There would be no victory monuments, and pigeons would have to find some other place.

The situation was intolerable.

Fortunately, man took things into his own hands.

The first thing he took into his own hands was either a club or a stone.[1] He may even have had a club in one hand and a stone in the other, an early instance of overkill.

The club and the stone were the first offensive weapons. The first defensive weapon was the skull, rapidly followed by the defensive club and the defensive stone. These were approximately the same size and shape as the offensive club and the offensive stone.

An important factor in early warfare was the cave. The person in the cave had the advantage over anyone entering the cave because his eyes were accustomed to the darkness. Once dark glasses were invented, this advantage no longer existed. But primitive man had no dark glasses. In fact he had no glasses of any kind, and this deprived him, if he had bad eyesight, of the opportunity of having his vision corrected to the standard that made him eligible for killing other people. When on the defensive, it also cost him the delay gained while saying, "Wait till I

---

[1] Teddy Roosevelt was not, as some think, the first to use the slogan "Carry a big stick."

take my glasses off," during which time his opponent might get out of the notion.

The earliest armed conflicts were probably between two men. Casualties were heavy, usually about 50 per cent. Women, children, and old people who stood around watching were called noncombatants and were in no danger whatsoever.

However, there was not as yet any such thing as war, war being armed conflict between nations. When one man kills another man it is murder, which is very different. Who ever heard of murder rallies, murder songs, murder bonds? Primitive man was too dim-witted to realize that if enough people could kill enough people it would no longer be murder, it would be war. Then, instead of being frowned upon, it would bring cheers and speeches.[1]

Another difference between murder and war is when and where they take place. Murder takes place in dark alleys and behind closed doors and when nobody is looking. War takes place on battlefields, out in the open, with newspaper reporters and photographers and even television cameras to record it. Obviously there is something sneaky about murder, as contrasted with war.

Primitive man, unaware of the moral and social advantages of war, nonetheless made some progress. Though he continued to kill in the old-fashioned way,

[1] It is a matter of taste, but there are those who prefer a long war to a long speech.

one person at a time, he made important advances in weaponry.

With the discovery of copper, iron, and other metals, he was able to construct weapons with sharp points and keen edges that had obvious advantages over the stone and the club. It was now possible to get rid of an opponent by thrusting a piece of metal through him. This was far easier and less time-consuming than beating him over the head. Even if the old method of beating over the head was resorted to, a piece of metal was not likely to break or splinter as a club sometimes did, to the embarrassment of everyone.

Invention of the wheel brought mobility. Instead of walking all the way to get within striking distance of his enemy, and being tired out on arrival, a man could ride there. Or, if he decided not to fight, he could get away faster than by running. Also, not getting out of breath, he could yell fiercely and even chant war songs, thereby contributing to the literary and musical arts.

Discovery of fire made it possible to go after one's enemy with a lighted torch and to burn the hair off his chest unless, of course, he was fleeing. It also made it possible to fight after dark, utilizing time that had previously been wasted in sleep.

Despite these encouraging developments, man was in a pretty sad state, warwise, for thousands of years.

CHAPTER II

The Beginnings of War

WHEN people began to group themselves in villages and tribes there was at last the necessary element of war: two sides. Now the people in one village could come together in a common cause, which was to overcome the people in another village. Or one tribe could annihilate another. People were rescued from the monotony of toiling in the fields. Men could get away from their wives. Life took on a new meaning.[1]

Gradually a warrior class emerged. These were professional soldiers, whose business it was to kill people on the other side professionally. There were no hard feelings about it; they were just doing a job. Even more detached were the professional soldiers known as mercenaries, who would kill people on either side, depending on who asked them first. Instead of fighting for honor, they fought for money, which was

[1] For one thing, for a great many people it was shorter.

something you could buy things with. Unlike the ordinary soldier, the mercenary knew what he was fighting for, and instead of looking forward to the end of the war looked forward to the first of the month.

Keeping pace with the development of war was the development of weaponry. The pointed stick was replaced by the sword and by the spear, the latter being a long stick with a sharp piece of metal on the end. The longer the stick, or shaft, the farther a warrior could stay away from his enemy, which was all right with him. Since a spear could be only about so long without becoming too unwieldy or too heavy to pick up, the length eventually became standardized. Finally, however, someone got the idea of throwing the spear, and this practice was taken up with great gusto. Early manuals on spear-throwing advise throwing (1) accurately and (2) first. Today a person might say "I have shot my bolt." In the early days he would have said "I have thrown my spear." To have thrown your spear and missed, when the other fellow still had his spear, was to have put yourself in an embarrassing situation.[1]

To get still farther away from the enemy, the bow and arrow were invented. The first arrows were probably tipped with flint, but arrows with metal tips

[1] Of course you might have a spare spear. Or you might throw yourself on your opponent's mercy, hoping it was not as sharp as his spear.

came shortly after. Once the metal tips were dipped in poison, men had their most effective weapon until the invention of gunpowder. Bows and arrows were first used to shoot animals. A survival of this practice is in the target used in modern archery, where the center is known as the bull's eye rather than the man's eye.

According to one source, "The origin of the bow and arrow is lost in the mists of antiquity." Not only the origin but many an arrow must have been lost back in those misty days. This is what Longfellow must have had in mind when he wrote the lines

> I shot an arrow into the air,
> It fell to earth, I knew not where.

The bowman of early days, aiming at a bowman who was aiming at him and about to let fly, was understandably nervous. He may even have trembled a bit. That, some etymologists think, is why the case of arrows on his back came to be known as a quiver.

To protect himself from the spear and the arrow, man at first simply held his arms in front of his head, but that left him vulnerable in the area of the heart and stomach. Or, if he held his arms over his heart and stomach, his head was wide open. Obviously, he did not have enough arms.[1]

So he invented the shield. This was at first made of

[1] Virgil recognized his dilemma in the opening line of the *Aeneid:* "Arms and the man I sing."

pieces of wood. Then the imaginative shieldmaker stretched over the wood the hides of animals which, having no shields and not even being able to raise their legs over their vulnerable parts, had proved easy prey to the spear and the arrow. As time went on, shields were decorated by signs, symbols, and faces of relatives, some of which were so frightening that an opponent would run when he got a look, without putting up a struggle. Other shields doubtless gave the address of next of kin, in case something went wrong. But finally military authorities cracked down, and soldiers decorating their shields were limited to their name, rank, and serial number. This was to foil enemy intelligence, which, along with intelligence of any kind, had for centuries been nothing to worry about.[1]

Another advance made in the pursuit of war was the domestication of the horse. Originally horses were wild.[2] They grazed, ran through the fields, and played an ancient game called mares and stallions. Never a thought entered their heads about making war or assisting anyone else make war.

Then men domesticated them. To domesticate is to tame, though literally it means to make feel at home. Horses failed to understand this, because they felt at

---

[1] The IQ test, as a factor in selecting young men for military service, would have been considered laughable in those days.

[2] This is not a term used in poker.

home in the fields, aimlessly wandering around, munching grass and flicking their tails. But men taught them to do useful things, such as pull a chariot carrying a warrior to the battlefield or haul a wagon full of corpses back from the battlefield. They even taught horses to carry a warrior on their back, right into the middle of a battle, with a good chance of being killed by a spear or an arrow.

Horses objected to becoming involved in wars which had nothing to do with the freedom or betterment of horses. They bucked and reared, making it hard for men, until they were finally subdued. Some think horses were the original conscientious objectors.

Thus it was that war and weaponry kept pace with other advances in civilization. Happily, by the time of the great empires and the great conquerors the means of conquest were at hand.

CHAPTER III

Egyptians, Assyrians, and Others

THE WHEEL, mentioned earlier, was one of the prime causes of war. Conflict came about when people in wagons and chariots invaded other lands and tried to take them over. If people had stayed home, or had had to walk, there would have been very few wars. However, without such wars there would have been little travel and the world would now be full of narrow-minded isolationists instead of broad-gauge warmongers. Wars have led to the subjugation of provinces, but they have had a beneficial effect in ridding us of provincialism.

One of the first to take a fortified city belonging to someone else was Thutmose III of Egypt, who became Pharaoh in 1501 B.C.[1] According to one his-

---

[1] Some give the date as 1481 B.C., when his wife, Hatsheput, the real ruler of Egypt, died. But Thutmose dated his reign from his marriage, in 1501 B.C., and once Hatsheput was dead there was no one to give him an argument.

torian, "Thutmose was a name to conjure with," and conjurers have been grateful ever since. Interestingly, Armageddon is the name of the place where according to prophesy the last great battle between good and evil (the Good Guys and the Bad Guys) will take place. But it was also one of the first cities captured by Thutmose.[1]

Modern imperialists owe a great deal to Thutmose. Besides taking over all the countries around him, he built up a fleet and established naval command over the eastern Mediterranean. His navy set a precedent by not only terrifying local rulers when his ships were sighted but affecting the economy of these countries. "The Egyptian fleet is in!" people would cry, and merchants would bring out their shoddiest merchandise to sell to the sailors, and fathers would lock up their daughters.

In modern times, wars have been fought for reasons that were sometimes unclear. But back in about 1375 B.C. people knew what they were fighting for. Under Amenhotep IV, Egyptians worshiped Aton, whereas most people in that part of the world worshiped Amon. The Egyptians were furious, considering Amon an impostor, if not a typographical error. The

[1] The city taken by Thutmose was Har-Megiddo, or Hill of Megiddo, later known as Armageddon. Like many conquerors, Thutmose may have thought he was fighting the last great battle instead of the first one.

struggle of Aton versus Amon went on for twenty-five years, with no telling how many lives lost. When finally Harmhab became Pharaoh and decided that the Egyptians might as well worship Amon after all, it was quite a letdown, and for a while there was nothing to fight about.

Egypt was divided into seven castes, of which the priests formed the first and the warriors the second. "We are second-caste citizens," the warriors some-times complained bitterly, but since there were five castes under them to lord it over and demand tribute from, they became reconciled to the system and man-aged to live with it.

Egyptians used mostly infantry, packed into a solid square about thirty deep, so close that the man in front was sometimes jabbed by the man behind, which was bad for morale. At the Battle of Thymbra, Croesus, who was as rich as Croesus and could afford anything, formed 10,000 Egyptian mercenaries in a square, 100 men wide and 100 deep. It took several days to deploy the troops because all the Egyptians wanted to be in the center. Or, if they were on the outside, and especially in the front, they wanted extra pay for hazardous duty.[1]

[1] The Battle of Thymbra took place in the sixth century B.C. and must be over by now, but I have been unable to find out how it came out. I have a feeling that Croesus lost. He may not have run out of money, but he ran out of Egyptians, or the Egyptians ran out on him.

Egyptian infantrymen were assisted by bowmen and slingers. Slingers were soldiers who used sling-shots and are not to be confused with those who had their arms in slings and happily journeyed to a billet behind the lines for rest and recreation, carefully keeping the pyramids between themselves and enemy action.

More effective as warriors than the Egyptians were the Assyrians, who in the ninth century B.C., under Ashurnasirpal II, established a vast empire that reached to the border of Egypt. The Assyrians were greatly helped by the fact that making war was their chief business. They realized that it is better to let other people work for centuries building up a civilization, and then take it over, than to go to all that senseless labor. Also warriors were in the top class, instead of priests. If priests wanted to participate in a campaign and get their share of the plunder, they could go along as chaplains, but they were to keep out of the way during the fighting. The Assyrians had learned that, though God was on their side, it was slow business praying your enemy to death.

The Assyrians went through rigorous training for battle, including fighting with wild beasts. Beneficial as this would be in basic training today, it would probably be frowned upon by the SPCA unless the contest was made more equal and the beasts, too, were armed.

While the Assyrians used mostly archers and spearmen, and gained mobility by the use of chariots, their chief weapon was terror. Once they had stormed a city, they sacked it, putting everything of value in sacks "to go." Most effective of all, however, was their treatment of prisoners, whom instead of killing outright they gave a choice. "Would you prefer to be impaled or flayed?" they asked considerately. No statistics are available concerning which of these methods was the more popular or what happened to those in the Undecided category.

As Byron has written in "The Destruction of Sennacherib," "The Assyrian came down like the wolf on the fold." Sennacherib was not a city the Assyrians destroyed but the leader of the Assyrians, and though he outnumbered the enemy when he attacked Jerusalem, he was badly defeated. Sennacherib, you see, forgot to have his soldiers inoculated for the plague, and they died like flies.[1]

Other fierce warriors in this early period were the Hittites, the Medes, the Babylonians, and the Chaldeans. Archers, we are told, were generally mounted; infantrymen were equipped with a small round shield and a short sword. Requests for larger shields and longer swords were turned down by planners, back in the capital. "What do you want with larger shields and longer swords?" they asked, never having been in combat themselves. Besides,

---

[1] If you have ever seen a fly die, you will know what an ignominious way this is to go.

they could not convert to the larger models until the oversupply of old ones was used up and factories were retooled.

Quite sensibly, battlefields in early times were agreed upon by both sides. The terrain was pleasant and open, and everything was made as comfortable as possible. It is not known whether the leaders of the two opposing armies tossed a coin to see which would start from which end of the field, but a bugle sounded the start of battle, and anyone who lunged forward before the signal was penalized five yards. There was an even more severe penalty for lunging in the opposite direction.

Warfare was becoming increasingly civilized. By 612 B.C., when the Assyrians were defeated at Nineveh by the Babylonians and Medes, prospects for killing on an even larger scale, and with less effort, were more promising than they had been for centuries.

CHAPTER IV

The Persians

As MANY historians have pointed out, in times of peace people sink into the idle pursuit of pleasure, and this in turn leads to indolence, purposelessness, and effeminacy. Fortunately, there is always some nation or people that keeps the world from following the degenerate ways of peace.

After the Assyrians had made their contribution, the Persians took over the responsibility of maintaining a healthful state of conflict. Under Cyrus, known as the first great conqueror, the Persians attacked and occupied most of the known world. As more of the world became known, other Persian leaders, such as Cambyses and Darius, conquered these portions.[1] Darius, especially, should be remembered for keeping the world in almost constant turmoil and/or subjugation. Opportunities for display of valor abounded,

[1] The best chance a nation had to keep from being conquered was to remain unknown.

and young men entering military service could be almost certain of rapid advancement and early death.

Unlike the Assyrians, the Persians did not lay waste the lands they conquered. Instead, they assigned a satrap to rule over them and, for obvious reasons, called these provinces satrapies. A satrapy was free to do anything it wished, as long as it was what the Persians wished it to do, and therefore rejoiced in its independence.

Darius, who was mathematically inclined, and especially enjoyed counting by tens, established the first Army division. This consisted of 10,000 men, made up of ten battalions of ten companies each. In each company there were ten sections. Before going into battle, Darius would personally count his forces, and woe betide any company commander, a little weak on arithmetic, who had nine sections, or eleven.[1]

Darius had a royal bodyguard which, by coincidence, consisted of 10,000 men. They were known as the "Immortals." If one of them died of natural causes, or was killed in battle, the fact was hushed up.

At the time the Persians were dominant in warfare, battles were chiefly fought between assaulting armies and fortified cities. Fortifications were impressive, the walls of Babylon, for instance, being 56 miles long, 85

[1] Some think Darius was the originator of the command "At-ten-*shun*," which in those day was accented on the second syllable.

feet wide, and 335 feet high. The Great Wall of China, though only 20 feet high, continued for 1400 miles, making up in length for what it lacked in height. On walls of this kind it was not necessary to put up a sign saying KEEP OUT. It should have been obvious to anyone that there was a desire for privacy.

But people were always trying to get in, seeming not to realize that they were unwanted. By the tenth century B.C. the Assyrians had built battering rams, which were mounted on wheeled wooden towers and protected in front by metal plates.[1] The Babylonians themselves, though objecting to having anyone beat on their own walls, used huge metal-tipped spears mounted on wheels, with which they poked at other people's fortifications. King Uzziah, in the eighth century B.C., placed catapults on top of towers and shot arrows and large stones over the walls of cities. The Greeks and Romans, whom we are coming to shortly, built fighting towers twenty stories high, which could be wheeled up to a wall. These permitted warriors to shoot arrows down on the defenders of a city and even, from one of the upper stories, to step onto the top of the wall. Pushing around a twenty-story building was no small feat, but amidst the excitement of war almost anything was possible.

Through the centuries it has been learned that

[1] "Something there is that doesn't love a wall," wrote Robert Frost, probably having a device of this sort in mind.

there is no wall that cannot be breached or gone around, unless the wall is made so thick that it becomes a solid square, with no room for people inside.[1] In the old days it was more difficult, when there was pride of workmanship, even on the part of slaves, and walls were really well built. One device used by assaulting forces was a tree trunk, covered with metal at the battering end, that was mounted on wheels and repeatedly banged against the wall. Camouflage being virtually unknown, the branches and leaves were usually removed. Had the greenery been left on, watchers from the battlements would have noticed nothing amiss until they felt the first impact, thinking it simply a tree that was growing from left to right instead of up and down.

One of the most interesting developments in weaponry, invented by the Egyptians but perfected by the Persians, was the scythe chariot. This was a chariot that had a double- or triple-bladed scythe sticking out to the side from the hub of each wheel. A warrior who saw a scythe chariot bearing down on him had a choice of being trampled on by the horses or, stepping to one side, having his legs cut off at the hips. Not having seen a Western movie, how could he know that the proper tactic is to seize the bridle of

---

[1] Following this principle, had the French built the Maginot Line so thick that it would have filled all the area from the German border to the Atlantic, they might have foiled the German attack in World War II.

the oncoming horses, swing oneself onto their backs, disarm the charioteer, and ride triumphantly into the sunset? Unfortunately, though the Persians often hired Egyptian mercenaries to do their fighting for them, they had no stunt men.

The scythe chariot was the first of a long line of combat weapons that were to have important peacetime uses. In this instance, the scythe chariot led to Cyrus [1] McCormick's invention of the reaper, patented in 1834,[2] which made possible great progress in farming throughout the world. The fortune amassed by McCormack led, among other things, to establishment of the McCormick Theological Seminary in Chicago. This is only one instance of the benefits of war.

And so we leave this great military era with a scythe.

[1] Or Scythrus.
[2] A.D., of course.

CHAPTER V

The Greeks

THOUGH the Greeks are known popularly for their poetry and art, their most magnificent achievements were made in the field of war. For one thing, they originated an ingenious form of war known as civil war, carried on for centuries among their city-states.[1] Previously one nation had warred against another, but the Greeks, who were forward-looking people, proved that it was possible for one part of a country to fight another, thus avoiding international complications and shortening supply lines.

The Greeks also invented the word *tyrant*, which was originally a perfectly good term applied to a ruler. If you called a tyrant a tyrant he took it as a compliment, because it meant he was No. 1 or The

[1] We have cities and we have states. The Greeks could never make up their minds.

Boss. It was an absolute term, however, and there was no such thing as an assistant tyrant or a tyrant junior grade.

The Greeks took warfare seriously. Every Athenian male was liable to military service between the ages of sixteen and sixty, and since very few lived to sixty in those days, many men died owing the State as much as fifteen or twenty years and, being patriots, were sorry as could be.

Of all the Greeks, none achieved such excellence in war as the Spartans. Spartans began military training when they were sixteen and spent all their life in the Army, turning over nonessential activities, such as law, medicine, business, and farming, to slaves.[1] The slaves were mostly Helots, whom the Spartans had conquered even though outnumbered twenty to one. Since the Helots resented a life of slavery and were often at the point of complaining, the Spartans declared war on them once a year, so they could kill any who were unhappy without breaking the strict Greek law against murder. The Spartans were not only physically fit but morally ingenious.

Most of a Spartan's education consisted of calisthenics and learning how to handle a weapon. An elementary class in spear-throwing could be pretty lively, with the teacher dodging and the blackboard

[1] Actually, as with other Greeks, their military service ended at sixty, at which time they were free to enter a trade or profession and start work.

becoming badly pitted. The three R's taught in Spartan schools were run, rassle, and riddle-your-enemy. It was the ambition of every young Spartan to be killed in battle and carried off on his shield. After carrying a heavy shield all day, as well as a sword and a spear, this was the life.

Unlike the Persians, who fought in large masses of troops, the Greeks liked single combat, man to man. For instance we read in the *Iliad* of combats between heroes like Achilles and Hector, with everyone else wisely staying out of it, except occasionally a god who, being immortal, ran no risk. The Greeks trained themselves as athletes to be ready for the demands of war. This was fortunate in the case of Achilles, who chased Hector three times around the walls of Troy without becoming winded.[1]

One of the greatest single combats of ancient times was that between Sohrab and Rustum, described by Matthew Arnold in the poem he imaginatively called "Sohrab and Rustum." Rustum killed Sohrab with a spear thrust, and you would have thought Rustum would have been happy. But Sohrab, who lingered through 334 lines, turned out to be Rustum's son, as the youth proved by baring a tattoo that his mother had thoughtfully pricked on his upper arm.[2]

---

[1] This was important, because otherwise Achilles would have been in no condition to give the speech that Homer had written for him.

[2] Such identification was later replaced by the dogtag.

But single combat, especially between the leaders of the opposing forces, eventually died out, along with the leaders. Once again, wars were fought between masses of soldiers, with the leader in a safe place. The Greek Army consisted of two types of foot troops. There were the hoplites, recruited from the upper classes, who were armed with pikes, swords, and shields, and were fairly well protected with helmets, breastplates, and greaves (armor that covered the shins, in case the enemy resorted to foul means, such as kicking). And then there were the psiloi, recruited from the poorer classes, who carried bows and slings but wore no armor. Greece, the birthplace of democracy, still had its social distinctions, as one of the psiloi, facing a volley of spears and arrows with no armor, would have told you.

The Greeks used cavalry, but there were no stirrups, since stirrups were not invented until about 550 A.D. Lacking stirrups, some cavalrymen just never could mount their horses, no matter how hard they tried, and had to content themselves with running alongside. What they felt the lack of even more was the stirrup cup, which would have given them a rousing sendoff, perhaps enabling them to leap clear over their steeds.

Like most armies in the early days, the Greeks employed the phalanx, which was a solid mass of troops commanded by a phalangiarch. Two phalanxes were commanded by a diphalangiarch and four phalanxes by a tetraphalangiarch, or four-star phalangiarch.[1] It was difficult for a phalanx to maneuver or even to keep in a straight line, from right to left and from front to rear. Despite the constant command "Dress right DRESS!" lines were sometimes pretty ragged. But it was hard for soldiers in the center of a phalanx to hear commands, as they shuffled along carrying their spears and glad there were no airplanes overhead. Indeed, soldiers in the center seldom saw action or much of anything else. But, packed together this way, there was a feeling of togetherness.

One of the innovations credited to the Greeks was the exaggeration of the size of enemy forces. At Marathon, for instance, the Greeks defeated perhaps 25,000 Persians, but by giving out the figure of 250,000 they made the victory ten times as impressive, and an important precedent was set. It was also at Marathon that the dissemination of favorable news made a significant advance. As soon as the Greeks won the battle, they sent their swiftest runner, Pheidippides, to Athens with the good news. He ran all the way, and when he stumbled into Athens, exhausted, he gasped out, "Rejoice. We conquer." This was enough for a headline but hardly satisfactory for a news story. Pheidippides, a better runner than foreign correspondent, was unable to amplify his

---

[1] No matter what it was, the Greeks had a word for it.

remarks, perhaps because, having spoken these few words, he fell dead. It was obvious that better ways of news gathering would have to be found.

Reference has been made above to the dedicated military training of the Spartans. This showed its worth in the battle of Thermopylae when, thanks to a Greek traitor who showed the Persians the way over a mountain trail to get at the Greeks from the rear, the Persians won a great victory. Among the 1400 Greeks, there were 300 Spartans, 700 Thespians,[1] and 400 Thebans. (No Lesbians, apparently.) The sole survivor was a Spartan, and the Spartans pointed to this with pride as justification of their lifetime of rigorous military service. Of course the one survivor might have been playing dead or hiding behind a boulder. But proponents of a military state still point to this as a shining example of Preparedness.

Having been defeated at Thermopylae, the Greeks took to the sea. The Battle of Salamis, in which the Greeks defeated the Persians, was the first great naval battle, and thereby set an Important Precedent. One reason for the Greek victory was their catching the Persian fleet in narrow waters. The Persians were soon in difficulty or, as we have come to say, in dire straits.

The Greeks used oarsmen to propel their ships.

[1] Unlike later Thespians, these did not limit their spear-holding to theatrical performances. As far back as Thermopylae they went into battle without makeup.

Since there were three banks of oarsmen, these ships were called triremes. In Latin, a remus is an oar, though it is also Romulus' twin brother and a folksy character who told stories about Br'er Rabbit. Ruins of Athenian shipyards reveal that four banks of oars were introduced about 330 B.C. Subsequently more and more banks were added, though after the oars got too high up to reach the water someone in the high command of the Athenian Navy, or possibly a tax-payer, called a halt.[1]

The chief device used in naval warfare by the Greeks and Romans was the ram,[2] a spur of hard-wood armored with iron or bronze that stuck out from the prow of the ship just under the water line and was used to poke holes in enemy vessels. If ramming a ship was not sufficient, hoplites hopped aboard and went to work on the crew with swords and pikes, making navigation difficult.[3]

For land warfare, Greece eventually developed the peltast, an infantryman with a short spear, a small shield, and light armor, well suited for mobility. Unfortunately, the peltast found it easier to run away than had his more heavily armed predecessors, and the Greeks had less and less success in the field. Moreover, from constant wars, mostly Greek fighting

---

[1] *I.e.,* put in his oar.

[2] Also called a rostrum, but anyone was ill-advised to stand on it, making a speech, during a naval engagement.

[3] A boarding party was not exactly filled with gaiety.

Greek, there was coming to be a shortage in that most essential of military supplies: people.

But as the Greeks declined militarily, at least they had someone to blame. The gods, they said bitterly, had let them down. In fact one Greek writer, Trygaeus, advanced the theory that the gods had moved away, out of range of prayers and without leaving a forwarding address. After hundreds of years of fighting, the Greeks were so disgusted that they thought of trying peace. It might not work, but it would be a change.

CHAPTER VI

The Macedonians:
Philip and Alexander

WARLIKE PEOPLE seem always to be sweeping down from the north. Apparently they want to get out of the cold, in addition to which there is no activity like swinging a sword or tossing a spear for giving the cheeks a rosy glow.[1]

In the fourth century B.C. the warlike people who swept down from the north were the Macedonians. At first they were led by Philip II, who rapidly conquered the Thebans and Greeks, thanks to his extensive use of cavalry and, even more important, his lengthening the Macedonian spear. According to Polybius, the Macedonian sarissa was 21 feet long, or a third again as long as the Greek pike.[2] How a

---

[1] Especially the cheeks of those hit by a sword or a spear.

[2] Historians say that 14 feet was as long as the Greek pike ever got, or the pike's peak.

Macedonian soldier could wield a 21-foot-long spear, or even lift it, was a military secret. "That's your problem" was about all a Macedonian recruit got from his sergeant.

Philip made other important contributions. He developed artillery, in the form of the catapult, which operated on the principle of torsion, and the ballista, which operated on the principle of tension. The tension of the ballista was partly in the device itself, which pulled back a projectile (usually a spear) by means of a windlass, and partly in the operator, who could never be sure whether it was going to work. The catapult and the ballista could hurl a projectile as much as 500 yards—unless, of course, the cord broke, which could prove a real disappointment to an artilleryman in about 350 B.C.

Philip also is to be remembered for forming the world's first standing army. Weighted down as a phalangite was, with shield and body armor weighing about 80 pounds, it is no wonder he was always wanting to sit, and this makes Philip's achievement all the greater.

The Greeks, though they outnumbered the Macedonians, fought valiantly. Their secret weapon was Demosthenes, who in a series of unflattering speeches against Philip, known as the *Philippics,* sought to undermine the confidence of the Macedonian leader. It was the first time, but not the last, that heavy oratory has been used against light artillery. However, it failed, since even the Greeks became bored.[1]

Even more successful as a leader of the Macedonians was Philip's son Alexander, who preferred to be known as Alexander the Great.[2] Instead of being pleased with his father's conquests, he wept bitterly. "My father will get ahead of me in everything, and will leave nothing great for me to do," he said, according to one biographer. But another writes that "Alexander carried out his father's dreams," and some of these were dillies, involving carnage, pillage, and wholesale slaughter.[3]

Alexander pioneered in the method of swift, unexpected movement. If possible, he captured the leader of the opposing forces, or caused him to flee. Usually he fled and, being the leader, was obediently followed by the rank and file, even though he kept shouting over his shoulder, "Go back and fight, you fools!" This is what happened in one of Alexander's great victories over the Persians, the battle of Issus, when, in the words of one historian, "Darius and his nobles took to their heels," though they also used their toes and any other way of getting out of there. Only the Greek mercenaries stood their ground, dying one by one. After all, they were getting paid for

[1] Orators, like rifles, come in large bore and small bore. Demosthenes must have been small bore, since he used pebbles in his mouth.

[2] Had he, too, been named Philip, it is hard to think of calling him Junior.

[3] Wholesale slaughter came in larger quantity than retail, and presumably cost less.

it. According to one account, more than 100,000 Persians were slain, as compared to 450 Macedonian losses. In war, these are considered favorable odds.

Alexander was, without doubt, one of the great generals of all times. Though the Greeks invented the word *strategy,* Alexander used it to defeat the Greeks. Not only his cunning but his strength was legendary. On one occasion he is said to have "thrown 30,000 horse over a river." Unless the horses were very light indeed, this was the achievement of no ordinary man.

As for crossing a river, he crossed the Jaxartes by having his men fill their tents with straw and sew them up, making rafts on which they floated toward the fierce Scythians on the other shore. Can you imagine how the Scythians felt when they saw a river full of tents? They became tense themselves. In fact they "broke and ran," though some who broke were unable to run or even crawl, and were easy prey for the Macedonians who, we are told, "set upon them." [1]

Nothing could stop Alexander. In open-field fighting he disposed his troops in two wings, a right wing and a left wing. Conservatives make much of the fact that Alexander gave his personal support to his right wing.

He also developed new tactics, as at the battle of

[1] Probably this should be "sat upon them," military historians being better at detecting tactical errors than grammatical errors.

Arbela, in using pincers. A Persian caught by Alexander's pincers, especially if he was caught in the right
place, screamed for mercy. He gave up his sword and
spear and sometimes, in his excitement, "threw down
his arms."

In attacking a fortified city, such as Tyre, Alexander used all known means to breach the wall and
invented a few devices of his own. One of the latter
was a mole he built across the water to this island city.
When the people within the city heard that Alexander was building a mole, they laughed, knowing a
mole was either a burrowing animal or a spot on the
skin described medically as a pigmentary nevus. But
Alexander had in mind the piece of masonry he built
200 feet wide from the mainland across the half-mile
strait. When Alexander came over this, with his
troops, horses, and chariots, were the Tyrians surprised!

Alexander was also one of the first to use mantelets to protect his attacking soldiers from missiles.
Mantelets were shields of wicker, covered with wood
or hide, that were mounted on wheels and pushed
along ahead of the soldier. They were more mobile
than foxholes, and took less digging, and one wonders
why they did not survive.

Of course Alexander himself did not survive, dying
at the ripe old age of thirty-two after conquering
everything from Greece to India.[1] Nor did his great

[1] He died of a fever. No one managed to kill *him*.

empire long survive. Alexander's generals, called the Successors, no doubt because of their military successes, fought each other for the next two decades, marching back and forth over Greece, Persia, and Asia Minor until things were pretty much as they were before Alexander started, except for more tombs. Mostly they were in search of gold, and their battle cry, long anticipating Keats, was "Booty is truth, truth booty!"

Unfortunately Alexander, though he would have been only fifty-two, was not around to note the outcome of his efforts as a world conqueror.

CHAPTER VII

Hannibal

From the time of Alexander to that of Caesar, probably no military leader was so successful in killing people as the Carthaginian, Hannibal. Hannibal's father also was a general, though his name, Hamilcar, has led many to think of him as an early form of transportation.

As has been pointed out, conquerors always sweep down from the north. Since Carthage was to the south of Italy, across the Mediterranean, it seemed no threat to Rome. However the wily Hannibal managed to sweep down from the north from the south, by going up through Spain, across Gaul, and over the Alps.

Much has been written of Hannibal's crossing the Alps with elephants. Actually his troops, numbering some 26,000, did not ride on the elephants, of which there were only thirty-seven.[1] The elephants were

[1] Of course about 700 soldiers might have got on the back of each elephant, but it would have been a bit crowded.

taken along to use in battle in the front lines, many a warrior feeling a little more secure with an elephant between the enemy and himself.[1]

In his battles in Italy, Hannibal was usually outnumbered. This caused him to use such underhanded devices as ambush and ruse. He would sometimes feint, or pretend to, but he was fully conscious when the enemy got within spear-thrust. Romans, who had not yet heard the expression "All's fair in love and war," severely criticized Hannibal for not announcing his arrival and sounding a bugle before battle as they did.[2]

The wars fought by the Carthaginians against the Romans were known as the Punic Wars. The word *Punic* was used by the Romans to refer to anything pertaining to Carthage, and it was not complimentary. What the Carthaginians called the Romans is not known, but even if it were it could not be printed here.

In one of his early battles in Italy, when he engaged the force led by Sempronius, we are told that Hannibal "fell upon his rear." Whether he slipped or tripped over something, we do not know, but he was

[1] Historians have overstressed the difficulty of Hannibal's getting elephants over the Alps. Hannibal had excellent supply lines, and a few extra peanuts were no problem to him.

[2] Notice should be taken of the fact that all the accounts of Hannibal were written by his enemies. What Hannibal needed in his Army was fewer elephants and more historians.

not seriously hurt, for he rallied his men and routed Sempronius.

Though Hannibal won many victories, such as the great battle of Cannae, he never succeeded in taking Rome. Instead of enveloping Italy, he was himself enveloped, which was not the way he intended it at all. Perhaps he knew, as one historian says, that "the intention of the Romans was slowly to strangle him," and this gave him an uncomfortable feeling in the throat. At one point he was "isolated in the toe of Italy," an embarrassing situation for a man of Hannibal's stature, and he did his best to become footloose again.

Ultimately he met crushing defeat by Scipio at the battle of Zama, his elephants having been frightened by the noise of Roman horns and trumpets, which were enough to terrify anyone, and "his Numidian horse" [1] having been driven from the field. When, at last, the Roman cavalry attacked Hannibal's rear, "the greater part of his men were cut down in their ranks; while of those who attempted to fly very few escaped with their life." The fact that any would attempt to fly, in 202 B.C., shows the desperation of the Carthaginian forces.

After sixteen years of fighting in Italy,[2] Hannibal

[1] Actually he had more than one.

[2] Some historians say seventeen years, some say eighteen. But sixteen seems long enough. It must have seemed even longer than that to Hannibal.

fled to Syria, Crete, and finally Bithynia. When the Romans pursued him even there, he managed to avoid falling into Roman hands. Cunning to the last, he took poison he had hidden in a secret place in a ring. Hannibal's career was a lesson to future conquerors, all of whom were well advised to affect a liking for jewelry.

CHAPTER VIII

The Romans

WARFARE reached a high point at the time of the Roman Empire. Instead of vague idealism, men knew what they were in the Army for: high pay, a share in loot, and excellent opportunities for sexual satisfaction through rape. When the motive of a war was something as simple as greed, it was easy for military and political leaders to explain. Everyone understood perfectly. Morals were low, but morale was high.

One important reason for fighting a war, to the Romans, was to acquire slaves. But for wars, the slave markets of Rome would have been short of merchandise. It would have been as hard to buy a slave as to find a watermelon in December. The need for slaves was not only a justification for war but a good reason for sparing the lives of able-bodied prisoners. There is no telling how many people, who would otherwise have been slaughtered, enjoyed a life of slavery instead.

Under the Romans, an important tactical change was from the phalanx to the more flexible legion. The Roman legion, with auxiliary troops attached, consisted of about 6000 men, making it a formidable force but considerably smaller than the American Legion. With their genius for organization, the Romans divided each legion into ten cohorts, each cohort into three maniples, and each maniple into two centuries.[1] The individual Roman soldier in turn divided an enemy soldier into two parts, the head and the body, with a single stroke of his sword.

Also revealing their love of classification, the Romans divided their soldiers into five classes, based upon their social position. The higher the social class, the heavier the armor.[2] Soldiers in the fifth class wore no armor whatsoever. Though they may have been more expendable, they were also more mobile, and in case of defeat could leave the battlefield faster than the more heavily armored nobility, and indeed sometimes ran neck and neck with the cavalry.

Not only this, but the Roman legion was often arrayed on the battlefield with the youngest men in

[1] This latter was not the enlistment period, though it probably seemed so to the average soldier. Actually, a century consisted of 100 men.

[2] This compares with the situation today: the higher the social class, the heavier the taxes.

the front and the oldest men in the rear. The fact that the leaders who worked this out were themselves older men was perhaps only a coincidence.

Though Roman soldiers used lances, pikes, javelins, and darts, the principal weapon was the *gladius,* a happy-sounding sword with a double-edged blade 20 inches long. It was used for both cutting and thrusting, not to mention whittling, during a pause in the battle, or performing an emergency appendectomy. It has been said that "it may be classed as the deadliest weapon in history," in view of the millions of men killed by it. What is not so well known is the fact that it gave its name to the gladiola or gladiolus, the lily with a sword-shaped leaf. A war between two armies, each armed with gladioli, would be colorful indeed.

The Romans, with their mechanical ingenuity, improved on the ballista and the catapult and invented the onager, literally the "wild ass," that threw or kicked a stone from a bag or wooden bucket.[1] The Romans also built roads, enabling them to get at the enemy and the enemy to get at them. But the greatest progress made by the Romans was in the field of digging, or of digging in the field. At the siege of Alesia in 52 B.C., Caesar's men shifted two million cubic meters of earth from trenches. Another Roman general, we are told, "dug a trench fifteen feet deep,

[1] Hence the expression "to kick the bucket," familiar to many foes of the Romans.

fifteen feet broad, and thirty-four miles long." It is presumed he had help. Those who say today, "This is a dirty war," should have been around in the first century B.C.

Gladiators (see the *gladius,* above) were employed as drillmasters, setting an example for the sergeants of modern times. Having performed for the public in the Colosseum, they were old hands at dramatizing the simple business of taking another's life. "Kill! Kill! Kill!" they would shout (in Latin, which was not yet a dead language), and soon they had even the rawest recruits [1] enthusiastically shouting "Kill! Kill! Kill!" and cutting and thrusting with their swords the while. It was an exciting scene, all these young men out in the open air getting wholesome exercise, their swords glinting in the sun.

Battles had previously been opened with the blowing of bugles, so that everyone would be awake and ready on both sides. The Romans, however, added what was called the *cohortatio,* an inspiring address by the commanding general. In the *cohortatio* a general would say stirring things about the national honor, personal bravery, manhood, the wickedness of the enemy, protection of home and family, the sacrifices of those who had gone before, and the prospects of loot. The *cohortatio* was sometimes so lengthy that

---

[1] Some were accidentally scraped by the swords of their inexperienced buddies.

soldiers, standing around holding shields, swords, pikes, javelins, and lances, were too tired, at the conclusion, to go into battle.[1] After giving the *cohortatio,* the general retired to a safe place and reshuffled his notes, preparatory to the next battle.

The Romans had a great military leader in Julius Caesar, who had the additional advantage of being a writer and thus, in his *Commentaries,* in a position to tell about his victories from his own point of view. In so doing he established a precedent for generals which still obtains.

Caesar conquered a large part of the world, beginning with Gaul, which he divided into three parts: Veni, Vidi, and Vici. His conquests took the Romans north to the Rhine and south to Egypt, and even into England, where for some reason (perhaps the bad weather or the bad cooking) they chose not to remain. In Gaul alone, the Romans under Caesar are said to have killed about two million persons, including women and children, which must have given their leader a sense of achievement.

Having accomplished so much against other peoples, Caesar saw no reason why he could not do as well at home. Thereupon he engaged Pompey in a struggle for power in Italy, and by defeating him proved himself equally competent at civil war. With so much success, it is no wonder he was made dictator for life and assassinated. Indeed very few dictators

[1] And, after applauding, they had all that gear to pick up.

have been so thoroughly assassinated, since he received more than twenty stab wounds from the daggers of men he considered his friends.[1]

After Caesar, the Emperor Augustus further expanded the Roman Empire and was responsible for an important military innovation. This was the creation of the Praetorian Guard, the Emperor's own private army. Dictators ever since have found such a force useful. Its soldiers can be kept loyal to the dictator rather than to the nation by the simple device of paying them directly. Knowing where the money is coming from helps clarify any confusion about loyalty. It is well to emphasize this regularly, perhaps once or twice a month, on what is known as Payday.

Eventually the Romans, having run out of countries to conquer, built walls along their frontiers and, as one historian says, "retired behind them." Many of the soldiers thus retired were only in their twenties or thirties, and this may have made the hard-working barbarians, on the other side of the wall, envious.

At any rate the barbarians, especially the Germans, were growing restive. The Romans had plundered their villages, and now, having got the idea from their enemy, the Germans decided to plunder the Romans. In the battle of the Teutoburger Wald the German

[1] One historian says, "He was stabbed in the end." But most pictures show him being stabbed in the chest and general area of the heart.

barbarians defeated the Roman legions under Varus and got their first taste of victory, which they liked. When Augustus learned what had happened, he did a strange thing. Unlike the distressed leaders of the past, who had always torn out their hair, Augustus, according to Suetonius, "let the hair of his head and beard grow for several months." As if this were not upsetting enough, especially to the imperial barber, he would sometimes thump his head against the doorposts, crying, "Quintilius Varus, give me back my legions!" Augustus was a bad loser.

For a time there was a period of peace, known as the *Pax Romana,* caused by the fact that the Romans had run out of opponents. Also everyone who seemed likely to make trouble was given citizenship in the Roman Empire. As the decree stated (in a rough translation from the Latin) : "If you can't lick 'em, get 'em to join you."

But under the emperors succeeding Augustus, as this unnatural condition of peace settled over the land, people became uneasy. They knew something was wrong, but couldn't put their finger on it. Except for building roads, walls, temples, and statues of the Emperor, there was nothing to do but eat. The Romans grew soft.[1] They went downhill.[2]

Meanwhile the barbarians, who had fought an uphill battle, grew hard. For instance there were the

[1] And round.

[2] With seven hills in Rome, this wasn't hard to do.

Alemanni, a virile German tribe whose name literally
means "all man." They rarely turned down a con-
script on the grounds of homosexuality. And there
were the Vandals, the Ostrogoths, and the Visigoths.
The Romans, who had been distracted from the
manly art of killing by such sensual pleasures as art,
music, and assorted orgies, were doomed. They made
a few feeble efforts to restore their leadership militarily. One was in 238 A.D., when the first floating
bridge was constructed to make it possible for Roman
soldiers to cross a river. It was made out of wine casks,
and the only trouble was that the casks first had to be
emptied, after which the soldiers were in no condition to cross the river.

Finally, in 410 A.D., Rome was sacked by Alaric and
his Visigoths, though historians fail to tell us how
many sacks it took.[1] Ironically, the barbarian Visigoths, who had become contaminated by Roman
culture, later fought the Huns, who were pure, un-
adulterated barbarians.

The Huns, it might be added, followed the his-
torical pattern and swept down from the north.

One lesson to be learned from the Romans is that
you should either keep fighting all the time or, when

[1] Everyone knows the name of Alaric. Not so many are
familiar with his predecessors, Fridigern and Athanaric, who
conquered the East Roman Empire and set things up for
Alaric. Even fewer are familiar with that great barbarian leader, Radagaisus, who is mentioned here for the sake of name-
droppers.

you stop fighting, get everyone else to stop. Another lesson is that no matter how barbaric you are, there is always someone else who is more barbaric. When you are trying to excel at something, such as being barbaric, this is discouraging. But do not give up. Rome wasn't burnt in a day.

CHAPTER IX

The Dark Ages

DURING the Dark Ages war, like other civilized pursuits, suffered a severe setback. The Romans, usually thought to have been conquered by the Goths and Vandals, according to one historian actually succumbed to Sloth and Apathy, which subsequently overcame the Goths and Vandals also.

For a time, the burden of carrying on war in Europe fell upon the Franks, a Teutonic tribe equipped largely [1] with the battle-ax, which could be either wielded or thrown.[2] Sometimes soldiers were armed only with clubs, and the long climb upward from the Stone Age, and all the military contributions of the Greeks and Romans, seemed futile indeed.

[1] Which at least is better than being equipped smally.
[2] The main thing was not to be indecisive, in the heat of battle, but to do one or the other—and quick.

The mobile Roman legion reverted to the solid square and the "human wall." The latter was used by Charles Martel (known by his men as "The Hammer" because of some of his wilder antics) to defeat the Arabs at the battle of Tours in 732. The Arabs took one look at the Franks, shoulder to shoulder like so many bricks, and withdrew from the field.

Though Charles Martel saved Christian civilization from being overwhelmed by the Moslems, which would have led to changes in architecture and no telling what else, many felt that the art of war had fallen on evil days, and mass killing was a thing of the past. Filled with nostalgia, they wistfully looked back to the Greek civil wars and the reign of Caesar, affectionately known as the Age of Slaughter.

But, though defeated by Charles Martel, the Arabs introduced a new element into warfare which was to have beneficial results. This was the zeal of a religious group to convert others to their faith. In addition to prospects of loot, Moslem soldiers were inspired by the thought that, as it says in the Koran, "The sword is the key to Heaven and Hell," and the quickest way to the Hereafter is by being killed in battle. Their opponents had the choice of being Moslems or dead, and some chose to live, not being very religious anyhow. By waging war successfully, Mohammed himself worked up from private to Prophet, which was the equivalent of Commander-in-Chief. Once, with a stroke of genius, he captured an entire tribe of Jews and "put 700 men to death in cold blood." [1]

Another effective device of Mohammed was to call his soldiers not GIs or doughboys or servicemen but True Believers. This has the same effect on morale as handing out Good Conduct Medals or giving solemn promises of being out of the trenches by Christmas.[2]

We cannot stress too much the contribution of the Arabs (Moslems, Mohammedans) in introducing the idea that wars should be waged in order to persuade others to change their religious faith. But for this, we might not have had the Crusades, the Thirty Years' War, or other conflicts which have enriched history and literature.

A valiant effort was made by Charlemagne to upgrade warfare. This great military leader of the Franks insisted that each proprietor of an estate send a warrior clad in a byrnie, or mail shirt.[3] Counts and great landowners had to produce retainers equipped with both a helm and a byrnie. No longer were peasant draftees permitted to turn up with nothing but fatigues and a club. Charlemagne insisted on quality. He saw to it that the men in his army arrived

---

[1] Sometimes, in his haste, he put his enemies to death while their blood was still warm.

[2] Which Christmas, of course, need not be specified.

[3] The femail shirt came later, with the WACs and, in abbreviated form, with entertainers of overseas troops.

with the basic equipment,[1] and then he further equipped them with shields, lances, swords, daggers, bows, quivers, spades, axes, picks, and iron-pointed stakes. In full gear, Charlemagne's men looked like traveling hardware salesmen, loaded down with samples.

The stirrup having been invented, Charlemagne made extensive use of cavalry, horses also being helpful in transporting the weaponry mentioned above. Charlemagne himself was dressed all in iron. According to a contemporary description at the battle of Pavia: "Then appeared the iron king, crowned with his iron helm, with sleeves of iron mail on his arms, his broad breast protected by an iron byrnie, an iron lance in his left hand, his right free to grasp his unconquered sword. His thighs were protected by iron greaves. His shield was plain iron, without device or color." The salesman who sold Charlemagne his outfit said, "It will wear like iron," and it did.[2] The only thing Charlemagne had to fear, other than the Lombards, Saxons, Saracens, and Avars, was rust.

So successful were the military campaigns of Charlemagne that he became Emperor over what is now Germany, France, Belgium, The Netherlands,

[1] For a while, before Charlemagne, all a new recruit had to have when he reported for duty was a head, two hands, and two feet, and these were counted none too carefully.

[2] Charlemagne, being seven feet tall, had to have everything tailored. Instead of a hand-me-down, he had a hand-me-up.

Switzerland, Hungary, most of Italy, and part of Spain. For a man who never learned to write, this proved that the sword is mightier than the pen.

On the death of Charlemagne his empire was divided among his sons and soon went the way (each son went his separate way) of the empires of Alexander and Hannibal. It was another example of the classic precept "Divide and be conquered."

A few more military exploits of the Dark Ages remain to be mentioned, eager though we are to get on to the Middle Ages, feudalism, and new forms of mass killing which, though not so effective as the methods of the Romans and Greeks, gave promise of better things to come.

There were the raids of the Norsemen, or Vikings, who, following the traditional method, swept down from the north. The first recorded Viking raid occurred in 799, shrewdly calculated to vex historians who prefer round numbers and yet feel uneasy when they say the Viking raids took place in the ninth century. The Vikings sailed in high-powered ships [1] and killed, stole, and burned wherever they landed. The sighting of Viking ships was not a cause for rejoicing.

The Vikings landed in the British Isles, sailed up the Seine to Paris, and traveled even as far as Russia and Constantinople. Whether the Vikings fought simply for the love of fighting, as some historians

[1] Which were probably responsible for what is called their "seafaring prowess."

contend, or were primarily interested in loot, is a matter of conjecture, but there is no reason to believe that the two motives are mutually exclusive. The Vikings proved that in war you can combine fun and profit, with travel thrown in as a bonus.

Once they landed, the Vikings used infantry tactics, and their principal weapon was the ax. The Norse ax was no ordinary ax. It had a heavy blade fixed to a handle five feet long. As one historian says, "Wielded with both hands, the heavy blade could cleave horse and rider at a blow." Occasionally a Viking, showing off, would wield his ax with one hand, but rarely could he get clear through the rider, much less the horse. His chief would reprimand him, saying "Two hands for beginners," and the Viking would be mortified and the horse would gallop off with only a nick in his neck.

Instead of armor, a Viking usually carried a kite-shaped shield, painted in bright colors. Opponents who saw a group of Vikings running toward them, apparently trying to get their kites into the air, were in for a surprise.

Then there were the Magyars, Asiatic tribesmen who suddenly came out of Hungary and made swift raids throughout Europe. They were mounted horse-men,[1] and their technique was to sweep across a province, load loot on their packhorses, set villages

[1] This means they were archers mounted on horses and not, except occasionally, over the fireplaces of their enemies.

afire, and get away before the defending forces could be recruited, armed, and trained. They can be compared to the American Indians and to the Russian Cossacks of a later period, though it really isn't necessary.

Finally, a word about the Norman Conquest, which pitted infantry and cavalry.[1] The English, under King Harold, still clung to their old military customs. They especially clung, for dear life, to the Saxon sword and spear. They were foot soldiers, walking to and running from battle. The Normans, however, were horsemen. "Why walk when you can ride?" they said, and the English kicked themselves for not thinking of it.[2]

At the Battle of Hastings, in 1066, King Harold had a larger force than Duke William, and a good defensive position on a wooded hill. But the British infantryman was no match for the Norman cavalryman, the British axman no match for the Norman bowman. There is some evidence that the British, in desperation, introduced aircraft, but if so, as one historian states, "The British wings were cut to pieces."

The Battle of Hastings marked the end of the heavily armed foot soldier, unless supported by cavalry. "The mailed horseman," we are told, with-

[1] In the end, it was the infantry who were the more pitted.
[2] This is easier to do when you are not on a horse.

out explanation of the postal system that made this possible, "emerged triumphant." [1]

A new era in warfare dawned. Henceforth anybody who was anybody, from William the Conqueror to Napoleon, rode a horse and looked down on lesser folk who walked. More important, bronze statues of conquering generals gave the generals something to sit on. Harold, the last of the Saxons, if depicted at all, is probably shown sitting on a rock, looking miserable. [2]

---

[1] Here is an interesting item concerning religion and weaponry. A bishop swung an iron mace at the Battle of Hastings because the rules of the Church forbade him to shed blood. It was all right, however, to crush a skull.

[2] How would you feel, if you had been shot in the eye by a Norman bowman?

CHAPTER X

The Crusades

M AN, it has been said, is the only creature on earth that will fight and die for an idea. During the Crusades, millions of persons took advantage of this opportunity.

The Crusades not only "opened the portals to life eternal" (i.e., killed) more people than at any time since the height of the Roman Empire, but also developed something without which many subsequent wars would not have been possible. This was propaganda, "the science of forging the idea into a weapon of war."

For several hundred years Christians had journeyed safely to Jerusalem, paying the Moslems only a small tax to visit the Christian shrines. But the fathers of the Church decided to embark on a Holy War. To get Christians into the proper frame of mind, papal bulls, bulletins (small bulls), letters, legends, and poems were sent all over Christendom, accusing the Saracens of such atrocities as overcharging tourists and poisoning the pepper exported from the Orient. It got so that people were afraid to use seasoning. One widely circulated painting showed a Moslem trampling on the True Cross, which in those days was the equivalent of the Flag. Indignation was rife. It became a moral issue, a matter of principle, to take Jerusalem. "Out with the infidels!" was the battle cry.

There were seven Crusades in all, over a period of some 200 years. Though this was before the invention of gunpowder, many Crusaders were, we are told, "fired by religious zeal," an effective propellant of the time. They also employed the crossbow, a combination of the cross and the bow which had both religious significance and killability. The great advantage of the crossbow over the ordinary bow was that it could be drawn ahead of time and kept drawn without physical strain to the archer while being aimed.[1] The crossbow was so lethal a weapon that Pope Innocent II in 1139 forbade its use as "hateful to God and unfit for Christians." Later this edict was modified slightly, when Christians were permitted to use the crossbow against Mohammedans. As time went on, Christians began to use it against one another.

---

[1] It was a crossbow that was used by Coleridge's Ancient Mariner to kill the albatross that was later hung around his neck. A Crusader could kill a Moslem without fear of any such gruesome reprisal.

This proves something or other about the banning of weapons that are too terrible to contemplate.

Richard Coeur de Lion, leader of one of the Crusades, was, by the way, killed by a crossbow. This was not during a Crusade to the Holy Land but while besieging a castle in France. King Richard should either have stayed home more (he spent only six months in England during the ten years of his reign) or ducked.

Other leaders of the Crusades included such colorful characters as Peter the Hermit and Walter the Penniless, neither of whom was known for his military bearing. Nor should we forget Dandalo, the Venetian, who besides being in his eighties was blind and could have retired on a full disability pension.

As for the Crusaders themselves, they were mostly individual volunteers, some of them full of religious zeal, some of them trying to get away from their creditors, and still others trying to get away from their wives. Many lost their lives on the way to the Holy Land, thanks to starvation, the plague, or inhospitable countrymen in the lands through which they traveled. Others survived all the hardships along the way and managed to be killed by the Saracens, which was a moral victory of sorts.

The fighting equipment of the Crusaders and their enemies was about the same, except that the Turks used a curved sword, or scimitar. Anyone hacked up by a scimitar was carried off to the nearest burial

ground, or scimitary. Communications consisted
largely of beacon fires, which informed anyone who
spotted them that something was up. Perhaps a city
was being burned. Perhaps an unsuccessful commander was being fired. There was also some use of
carrier pigeons by the Turks when they were besieged
in Acre, though there was always the question of
whether to send a pigeon out with a message or, as the
siege lingered on, to make pigeon pie.

Despite all obstacles, the city of Jerusalem fell to
the Crusaders in 1099. No sooner did it fall than it
was razed. The slaughter by the Christians has been
described as one of the bloodiest in military chroni-
cles. According to one historian, the victorious Crusaders "literally waded in gore," and many of them
had forgotten to bring overshoes. The March to the
Holy Sepulchre has been compared to "treading out
the wine-press," which gives the general idea.[1] It was
a Great Victory for the Western World.

It must not be thought, however, that the Christians were bloodthirsty or lacking in consideration
for the enemy. There were rules of warfare. There
were codes of honor. There was sportsmanship. For
instance, according to the *Treva Dei,* or Truce of
God, all warfare was suspended from noon on Satur-
day until dawn on Monday. Later, this truce was extended from Wednesday evening to Monday morn-
ing, making it a nice long week end. Someone had the

---

[1] Instead of seeds, however, there were bones.

idea of extending the truce still further, from Monday to Monday, but this never went through. There had to be *some* time for fighting. You couldn't depend entirely on the plague to keep the population down.[1]

Though millions lost their lives during the Crusades, the Moslems kept taking Jerusalem back. After the seventh Crusade, with Jerusalem once more firmly in Mohammedan hands, it was hard to get up any enthusiasm for having another go at it. Even atrocity stories had lost their zing. "There must be someone closer to conquer," people said, "and save that long trip."

The Crusades were not a total loss. Christians who survived brought back silks, embroidery, and knick-nacks that made excellent conversation pieces. And they learned important military lessons, for instance that in tropical lands it is impractical to wear heavy armor, at least without an antiperspirant.

Frederick Barbarossa, Emperor of the Holy Roman Empire and one of the leaders of the Third Crusade, learned another lesson, important to military leaders since his time. To wit, even an Emperor is unable to walk on water, no matter how much he may be encouraged by the huzzas of his men. Frederick drowned while crossing a river in Cilicia, Asia Minor.

[1] Moreover someone (perhaps a maker of swords) pointed out that any lengthening of the truce would have an adverse effect on the economy.

CHAPTER XI

The Age of Chivalry

ANOTHER term for the Middle Ages is the Age of
Chivalry. The word *chivalry* is related to *cheva-lier* or "cavalier" and means horseman. A horseman,
in turn, means not someone who is part horse and
part man but someone who rides on a horse. Anyone
who rode on a horse was not only in a higher bracket
than those who walked [1] but, in battle, considerably
safer. Something of the same distinction remains today between the motorist and the pedestrian.

Mostly those who rode horses were knights. It was
not easy to become a knight. First, at the age of seven,
you became a page, running errands and being taught
music, dancing, hunting, and the use of arms.[2] At
about fourteen, if you had done your work well and
were not a dropout, you became a squire, which

[1] Two or three feet higher, and slightly bowlegged.

[2] In those days, before the frug and the watusi, arms were
used in dancing too.

[62]

entitled you to go along with a knight at battles and carry his spare lance and do helpful little things such as pound the dents of his shield. At twenty-one, you were struck on the neck by your liege lord, who used the flat side of his sword and said, "I dub thee knight." What was exciting about this ceremony was that the liege lord might really dub, or slice, and take out a large divot.[1]

For several centuries, most of the fighting was done by knights. Only knights could afford a horse and a complete set of armor, which in those days was said to be worth the price of a small farm.[2] When a knight rode off to battle, the serfs gave him a rousing cheer and went back to their hoeing. "Take that!" they would say to a weed, imagining it to be a Saracen. A serf lived a hard life, but, not being considered fit for combat, often lived longer than a knight.

Knights always fought for a Cause. Usually, we are told, they thought "they were doing God's work," God apparently being too busy to do it himself. When unable to convert Unbelievers to Believers, they converted them from Living to Dead. They also fought for their liege lord, who sent them forth with some such inspiring message as "Go out there and fight."

[1] "Good knight!" he would then exclaim in dismay.
[2] Comparable to the modern alternative "guns or butter" was "armor or a farm."

A knight also fought for his ladylove. As soon as she showed some sign of interest, such as dropping her handkerchief or her eyes, he departed on an adventure of knight-errantry, often staying away several years to show how much he loved her. Each time he killed someone, he dedicated the corpse to his ladylove, knowing how pleased she would be.[1]

When not out on a military expedition, knights practiced in tournaments, where they jousted by riding full speed at one another with an outstretched spear or lance. This was called tilting, and some knights tilted a little too far and fell off. It was excellent preparation for war, and good fun for the spectators, who loved the clatter of lance against shield and the thud of a body against the ground. Tournaments not only helped knights get ready for war but made possible books like Sir Walter Scott's *Ivanhoe*.

To protect himself against the pike and the crossbow, the knight shifted from mail to armor plate. Heavily armored from head to feet, he was virtually immune to attack.[2] The only problem was to hoist him atop a horse and to develop a strain of horses that could stand the strain.[3] Eventually, as James I of England ironically observed about all this iron,

[1] There is no evidence that a knight cut off the ears and presented them to his ladylove, in the manner of more imaginative bullfighters of today.

[2] This was before invention of the can opener.

[3] From carrying the nobility, horses developed lordosis, or swayback.

"Armor provided double protection—first it kept a knight from being injured, and second, it kept him from injuring anybody else."

But for the longbow, and then gunpowder, wars might have come to an end in the thirteenth century, with knights clanking around harmlessly. But, fortunately, something always turns up.

Be of good cheer, and wait a few more pages.

CHAPTER XII

The Mongols

So WAR for a time lagged in the Western world, with knights almost immobilized in their heavy suits of armor, or taking refuge in castles surrounded by turreted walls, moats, and signs saying KEEP OUTE.[1] For excitement, bloodshed, and derring-do, we must turn to Asia.

When he was only thirteen, Genghis Khan succeeded his father as chief of a small Mongol tribe. He soon proved that he was a military genius by winning the Tatars to his side, perhaps because he knew enough not to call them Tartars, as many have done since.[2] After many campaigns, he conquered a large

[1] Actually the keep was in, this being the central and most fortified part of the castle, sometimes called the donjon.

[2] The word Tartar for Tatar resulted from confusion with Tartarus, the infernal regions where the spirits of the wicked were consigned for punishment. Naturally any Tatar, especially if he had read the *Iliad,* disliked being connected with Hades.

part of the world, including most of what is now China and Russia. He claimed that he had a divine call, which made soldiers who followed him into battle feel almost as if they were going to church.

One of the significant military developments of the Mongols was the use of spies and secret agents. These went ahead of the main force and promised all manner of kindness and rewards to the people of a besieged city. It was always a surprise to these trusting people, when they opened their gates and put out Welcome mats, to find themselves set upon and butchered. Many considered this dishonest, but they were too dead to make any effective protest.

The military success of the Mongols was owed largely to their horsemanship and mobility. They would sweep down and be gone again before their enemy knew what had hit them, though they suspected it was someone unfriendly. The Mongols used the bow and scimitar, as well as a new type of lance, equipped with a hook for dragging one's adversary out of the saddle. "What will they think of next?" an unhorsed horseman would mutter sadly, meanwhile shaking his head (to see whether it was still on) .[1]

One of the most interesting facts about Mongol bowmen is that they used arrows of different calibers for different purposes. Thus they used an arrow of

[1] Some see this as the origin of polo. After all, Marco Polo visited China about this time. Be this as it may, the Mongols must be credited with bringing sport back into warfare.

one size on a horse, a smaller one on a man, and a still smaller one on a child, when they were shooting up a town. They probably had an arrow of very small caliber for shooting a fly, before invention of the fly swatter, and the squinty eyes of the Mongol probably resulted from years of taking aim.

Despite all their successes, the Mongols had the good sense to quit when they were ahead and to withdraw with their booty when they felt they had gone far enough. Napoleon could have learned something from Genghis Khan, Kublai Khan, and Tamerlane.[1]

---

[1] Tamerlane, it is true, almost went too far, but he died of fever in the nick of time. A conqueror who dies a natural death before being defeated in battle shows good judgment.

CHAPTER XIII

The Hundred Years' War

Historians speak of the Hundred Years' War,[1] although it actually lasted 116 years (1337–1453). Whether one believes in round numbers or in precise accuracy, the war set a record for length which has never been equaled. In truth, the Hundred Years' War was a series of wars with truces and treaties in between to enable the antagonists to gather strength for the next encounter. It is very hard for the average soldier to fight a hundred years without a break.

The Hundred Years' War was fought for a higher purpose than most wars. It was fought over [2] France, which the English claimed because England had been conquered by a Frenchman, William of Normandy, in 1066. It took them 271 years to realize that because

[1] Or the Hundred Years War. Whether the apostrophe is essential has led to the formation of two schools of thought and several duels between military historians.

[2] In fact all over.

William had conquered England and become their king, the King of England should also be the King of France. Another way of looking at it was that since a Frenchman had conquered England, the King of France should be the King of England. The French, who took a narrow, nationalistic view, which, had it prevailed, would have cost us the Hundred Years' War, believed that the King of France should be the King of France and the King of England should be the King of England. To any thinking person,[1] this was patently absurd and further evidence that you can never trust the French, who use a sly, devious way of rationalizing which they refer to as logic.

Another thing that brought on the war was the fact that both the French and the English claimed the English Channel. Anyone who has ever crossed it in rough seas, and been deathly sick, will wonder that this body of water should be considered worth fighting for.[2]

Some idea of the length of the Hundred Years' War may be gained from its having extended over the reigns of five English kings and five French kings.

[1] Such as King Edward III.

[2] See Alexander Pope's "What mighty contests rise from trivial things." Pope had in mind the theft of a lock of hair, clipped from the head of Belinda (Miss Arabella Fermor) by "a two-edged weapon," also referred to as "the glittering forfex" and "the fatal engine." Pope's "The Rape of the Lock" is an excellent source for the study of war and weaponry.

Fortunately, kings were in office for life, and it was not necessary for them to make the war in France a campaign issue, with people clamoring "Get the war over and bring our boys home." It was also fortunate for King Edward III of England, who started the war, that he did not know how long it was going to last. Even the most stout-hearted English soldiers might have been taken aback, perhaps all the way aback to England, had they known the war would last one hundred (or 116) years.

Thanks largely to the longbow, the English won a great victory over the French in the Battle of Crécy. The French outnumbered the English by more than two to one, but they had only the crossbow, which was no match for the English weapon. The longbow was from six feet to six feet seven inches in length, and was generally made of yew.[1] It could shoot a 37-inch arrow that would pierce chain mail or kill a horse at two hundred yards. At closer range it could make an arrow penetrate "ordinary plate armor, two layers of mail armor, or a stout oaken door." The English bowman had to be pretty stout, too, to handle a bow taller than himself. In a new military tactic, he dismounted from his horse to wield his longbow. Aiming his arrow and pulling back the bowstring on a bow taller than himself was a full-time occupation.

The longbow was a gratifying advance in the long

[1] This led to the battle cry "Yew-hoo!"

history of weaponry. There are some rousing descriptions of its accuracy and penetration [1] at the Battle of Crécy. "Fully armored French knights were pinned to their horses," we read in one account. In another, "The English archers pierced enemy breastplates and pinned helmets to heads." A French soldier, with his helmet pinned to his head, suffered not a little embarrassment when he entered a house and was unable to take his hat off.

Another great victory by the English was at the Battle of Agincourt, in 1415. It was fought, according to Shakespeare in *King Henry V,* because the young king was sent a box of tennis balls by the Dauphin of France. To Henry, this was not cricket. By the end of the fourth act he had killed ten thousand French soldiers, while losing only twenty-nine of his own men. [2]

But if the English had the longbow, the French had Joan of Arc, a simple peasant girl who by raising the siege of Orléans and leading her people to victory after victory proved that it is unnecessary for a field commander to have any military training. True, she was captured and burned at the stake, but this was because the English thought her not a war criminal but a witch.

By the end of the Hundred Years' War the English had been driven out of all of France except the port

[1] Written by penetrating historians.
[2] Shakespeare makes it more dramatic.

city of Calais. At least from the English point of view, it might be questioned whether the war had been worth the effort. But as we can see now, with the perspective of history, it was worth every bit of the destruction and all of the lives lost. In addition to development of the longbow, it had put an end to feudalism by creating national armies, in which soldiers received a fixed and regular wage as well as a share of the plunder.[1] Military service became attractive as a career and was a duty for the ordinary citizen rather than a prerogative of aristocracy.

Long as it had taken, the Hundred Years' War had proved an important point. War is for everybody.

[1] That is, salary and commission, even for noncommissioned officers.

CHAPTER XIV

The Coming of Gunpowder

FOR A TIME the longbow was considered the ultimate weapon. It was not, however, even the penultimate weapon, as developments in the fourteenth and fifteenth centuries were to prove. With the coming of gunpowder, the art of killing made its most spectacular advance until recent times. Everyone was thrilled to death, even though few could foresee that these humble beginnings in explosives would lead eventually to the invention of dynamite and the establishment of the Nobel Peace Prize.

Gunpowder was not without competition. The Black Death, or bubonic plague, for a time was more effective. According to one historian, this great disease "carried off a quarter of the population of Europe." And, though our historian neglects to say so, it failed to bring them back. Had someone been able to package the Black Death and use it as a weapon,[1] gunpowder might have been unnecessary.

Some believe that the Chinese invented gunpowder before 225 B.C. But, uninspired by democratic ideals or the Christian ethic, the Chinese missed their great opportunity. Instead of using gunpowder to make war on their neighbors, they employed it only in fire-crackers, taking childish satisfaction in the noise. They also may have used it to propel rockets, but merely because they enjoyed the spectacle. If only someone could have told them how to get some good out of their gunpowder instead of burning it up frivolously! [2]

In the Western world, gunpowder seems to have been discovered by Roger Bacon, who in 1249 wrote about it in his exciting book, *Epistolae de Secretis Operibus Artis et Naturae et de Nullitate Magiae*.[3] Bacon apparently tried to keep his discovery of gunpowder a secret, perhaps because he was a Doctor of Theology and not a Ph.D. Unlike the true scientist, he was squeamish about an invention that might be used to kill people.

Even if Bacon invented gunpowder, he did nothing to connect this substance with firearms. As an emi-

[1] Thanks to remarkable progress in science, we now have the possibility of germ warfare.

[2] But at this time there were no military advisers in China, sent by more enlightened and technologically advanced nations.

[3] Which I confess I have not read. I have been waiting for the movie.

nent military historian says, "Who first thought of propelling a ball through a metal tube by exploding gunpowder is unknown." The reason may be that the first time this unknown inventor tried it he put in a little too much gunpowder, and the thing exploded in his face. After this, even close friends failed to recognize him.

The first "guns with powder" were imported into England from Ghent in 1314, starting a long tradition of shipping arms from one country (to make money) to another country (to make trouble). The earliest weapons using gunpowder were shaped like vases or pots. The man who lit one of these things was usually either very brave or very fleet of foot, or both. After lighting the device, he himself lit out for someplace as far away as possible. These wide-mouthed pieces were effective solely for battering at doors and walls from very close ranges, and caused extensive loss of life only when they exploded and killed the gun crew. Some spectators were killed by the concussion when, as they stood there holding a finger in each ear, their two fingers were driven into their heads until they met.

The forerunner of the cannon was the bombard, which was made of brass or copper and later of iron. The bombard was, we suspect, used for bombarding. For many years the shot fired by a bombard was solid, and often of stone. A bombard known as Mons Meg (see, later, Big Bertha) had a bore of 20 inches and fired a stone ball weighing 300 pounds. A missile of this sort was large enough to be noticed and, if one kept one's eyes open,[1] could be dodged. It did not explode, and the best defensive tactic was just to let it roll on by.

But soon someone got the idea of using hollow shells which exploded on contact and scattered fragments of iron and flint through the air. Dodging became more difficult. Indeed, incendiary shells and red-hot shot[2] were in use before 1470, and these soon had people dancing in the streets.

Bombards were at first fired from mounds of earth. Then they were placed on sledges. By the middle of the fifteenth century they were mounted on wheels and could be drawn by horses.[3] Now they could move about with the army, and we have the beginnings of artillery and of caissons which when not being used to carry ammunition could be used to carry a body in a funeral procession. A dual-purpose vehicle such as this, employed both in killing and in disposing of the dead, was a joy to persons responsible for military budgets. Often they could be heard happily humming, "And those caissons go rolling along."

Probably the most important use of bombards until modern times was in the siege of Constanti-

[1] Otherwise one's eyes were closed permanently.

[2] There is something catchy about "red-hot shot," when you say it over and over and get the right beat.

[3] The earliest pictures of them, however, were drawn by men.

nople by Mohammed II. The fall of the city, in 1453, was in no small part brought about by Mohammed's use of siege guns, including a super-bombard called Basilica which had a 36-inch bore, was so heavy it required 200 men and 60 oxen to move it, took more than an hour to load, and fired a ball that weighed 1600 pounds [1] and traveled for more than a mile. Though the Basilica fell apart after the first few shots, so did the defenders of the city, who were terrified by this artillery monster. According to a contemporary account, it "belched fire," no doubt because the gunpowder used by the Turks contained more sulphur and saltpeter than bicarbonate of soda.

The first hand-gun resembled a small cannon on a straight stock which could be carried and fired by one man. It weighed about ten pounds and was fired by applying a slow-burning match to powder in what was rather graphically called the touchhole. It was touch and go. Or rather, since unlike the igniter of the bombard this early rifleman was unable to depart, it was stay and pray.

The Spanish seem to have devised the matchlock, or arquebus, which could be fired by squeezing a trigger. A smoldering match was still used, but when the trigger was pressed the match was dipped into the gunpowder by a clamp (serpentine), something like the hammer of a modern gun. The great advantage of

[1] In another book it says 800 pounds. I bring this up not to question the accuracy of historians but to show that I have read more than one book.

the matchlock was that the soldier could focus on the target instead of looking for the touchhole. Marksmanship improved markedly.[1]

The only trouble with the matchlock was that firing it required ninety-six separate motions, including measuring the powder and pouring it down the muzzle, dropping in the lead ball, covering it with a wad of rag, uncovering the priming pan, pouring in fine-grained powder, closing the priming pan, adjusting the match in the serpentine, opening the cover of the priming pan, and squeezing the trigger. The gunner hoped his target would hold still while all this was going on.[2]

Gunpowder brought an end to the Middle Ages and a large number of people of all ages. As one historian states, having in mind that it made the prince and the peasant equal, "Gunpowder was a great leveling factor." Persons pierced by an iron ball, however crudely fashioned, were prone to agree. If they were not dead, they were in trouble and willing to admit it.

It may be said, in short, that the Middle Ages ended with both a bang and a whimper.

---

[1] Great was the relief of soldiers to the left and right of the arquebusier. They had been watching nervously as his hand-gun wobbled around while he looked for the touchhole.

[2] A faulty firing, in which there was a small explosion but no ejection of the ball, was known as "a flash in the pan." This is the truth.

CHAPTER XV

The Renaissance

G UNPOWDER, together with other contributions of science to warfare, did much to create the hole man of the Renaissance. During this exciting period, spirits were lifted. Heads were sometimes lifted, too, though this was more hazardous, with the air full of bullets.

The great military power in the sixteenth century was Spain, which under Charles V occupied territory even greater than the lands once dominated by Charlemagne. The Spanish success was due in part to its balance of pikemen and arquebusiers, the pikemen holding off the enemy while the arquebusiers reloaded.[1] In part it was due to Spanish solicitude for the soldier's soul. In each *tercio,* a tactical unit of

---

[1] As late as 1600 it still took ten to fifteen minutes to load and fire an arquebus. Still, there was a certain status in wielding a hand-gun, and many a father said to his son, "Don't be a piker."

about 3000 men, there were thirteen chaplains, as against a medical staff consisting of one surgeon and one physician. When a wounded soldier called for a doctor, the chances were better than six to one that he would get a D.D. instead of an M.D.

Italy of this period has been compared to ancient Greece, with its great artistic achievements nicely balanced by incessant warfare, usually civil war among the various city-states. Even an artist like Leonardo da Vinci was not too busy painting to do something useful, such as designing a mortar, a submarine, or a flying machine. Some Italian arquebuses were works of art, so beautifully decorated that it was a privilege to be shot by one of them.

Gradually the musket came to replace the arquebus.[1] The only trouble with the musket was that it was so heavy it had to be supported on a forked rest or crutch. Not until Gustavus Adolphus, in the seventeenth century, was the musket made light enough that the crutch could be dispensed with. It was a great day when Gustavus Adolphus gave the order to his men, "Throw away your crutches." Although he will be discussed in the next chapter, we cannot wait to say that it was also Gustavus Adolphus who introduced the wheel lock, a forerunner of the flintlock. By throwing off sparks that ignited the powder in a gun, it did away with the necessity of

[1] And with the musket came the musketeer, without whom Alexandre Dumas would have been sadly handicapped.

applying a match each time. It was as important to a soldier in those days as a cigarette lighter is to a smoker today.[1]

The pistol, a small arquebus about two feet long, was invented around 1540 by an Italian named Vitelli. Interestingly, he was a native of Pistoia. The word *pistol*, however, comes from a Czech word meaning "to peep," and it is hard to see the connection unless the person who coined the word thought someone was merely peeping at him through the barrel and was surprised when his brains were blown out.[2] The pistol enabled a horseman to fire while at full gallop, thus greatly speeding up warfare. Since he usually missed his target, casualties for a time declined alarmingly, though the fun element of war was as great as ever and, for some,[3] even greater.

Profoundly disturbing to those who feared a slackening in loss of life was the fact that the Black Plague died out. But replacements were at hand. Diseases such as smallpox and syphilis were carried by soldiers to all parts of the world. Save for wars of conquest, these diseases might have been unknown in many countries, which through complacency would have remained backward in medical science. As for syphilis, some say it was brought back from the New World

---

[1] Imagine a soldier, before the invention of the wheel lock, caught in battle without a match.

[2] There is also a "pistil," a rather sexy word to a flower, which is found in the phrase "as hot as a pistil."

[3] Cowards, who preferred to go on living.

by Columbus' sailors. If this is true, syphilis was the first of many useful imports from America, to be followed by tobacco, the potato, and Coca-Cola.

While the Spanish, French, and Italians are given most of the credit for continuing and improving upon warfare in the sixteenth century, we should not forget the Swiss. At this time the Swiss, later to decline to such peaceable pursuits as yodeling and hotelkeeping, made their living as mercenaries.[1] According to one historian, "The Swiss, finding profit a more compelling motive than patriotism, developed a large and formidable army which remained at the call of any royal bidder." After a little bargaining, soldiers would fight equally well for the French, Italians, or any other employer. They might even change sides in the middle of a battle, if the price was right. The Swiss, says this same historian, learned "a military pride which combined the stoutest courage with avarice, truculence, and revolting butcheries of prisoners." They were, in short, real professionals.

Many as were the land battles at this time, the most spectacular were at sea. Spain, Venice, and the Papal States formed the Holy League[2] to fight the Turks. Spain entered the League to protect her own coasts and shipping. Venice came in to regain Cyprus from the Turks. All three asserted that they were making

---

[1] Some see no great change from the Renaissance mercenary to the modern hotelkeeper.

[2] Seldom have military powers, joining forces to begin a campaign of conquest and destruction, been so aptly named.

war on Turkey "to save Christianity and protect humanity," which seemed reasonable enough.

As in the Crusades, the morality of the other side was shown to be despicable. For instance, it was reported that a Venetian leader in Cyprus, after having his ears and nose cut off, was hoisted to the yardarm of the Pasha's galley and flayed alive. Then his skin, stuffed with straw, was paraded in the streets. As can be imagined, this made the Christians very, very angry. "We'll show those Moslems," they muttered, sharpening their knives, preparing their flaying instruments, and placing some hay in their knapsacks. Some even said, "We'll show them a thing or two," intimating that they were familiar with a few methods of torture unknown as yet by the less advanced Moslems.

The Holy League fleet met the Turks in the famous Battle of Lepanto in 1571. Consisting of 316 ships,[1] it was the greatest Christian fleet that had ever been assembled in the Mediterranean. Its galleys were propelled by fifty-four oars, twenty-seven on a side, manned by slaves chained to benches. Boatswains, pacing up and down the gangway, increased the beat by flogging the slaves into a frenzy.[2]

[1] Another source says 200. Still another, hedging, says "around 300." Who is to be believed? This is the kind of thing that makes you wonder about historians.

[2] They were careful not to flog them into unconsciousness. A musically inclined boatswain might, while flogging, gently sing "Row, row, row your boat" to encourage the slaves to greater effort.

The ships of the Holy League and those of the Turks engaged in combat and soon were bound together by grappling irons. Soldiers then boarded enemy ships and fought on the decks in what has been described as "battles of infantry on ships." They might as well have fought on land, where it would not have been so crowded, but then this would not have been the most decisive naval engagement since Actium in 31 B.C.

Eventually the Christians won, losing a mere seventeen ships and 7500 dead. It was the last battle of oar-driven ships and hand-to-hand fighting. Speaking of hands, we might add that one of those fighting on the Christian side was Cervantes, who lost his left hand. Though this did not keep him from writing *Don Quixote,* he was understandably annoyed by writers who sneered, "I could have written it with my left hand." [1]

Seventeen years after the Battle of Lepanto came the second great naval battle of the century. This was between the Spanish Armada and the English fleet in 1588. The Spanish hoped to invade England to get back at the English because of the raids on Spanish

[1] My story is spoiled by the article in the *Encyclopedia Britannica* (11th ed.), which says that a shot "permanently maimed his *right* hand." But General Mitchell, in his *Outlines of the World's Military History,* p. 272, says Cervantes "lost his left hand." And Bernard and Fawn Brodie, in *From Crossbow to H-Bomb,* p. 10, also say it was his left hand. That makes it two to one that left is right.

ships made by Sir Francis Drake. They were also annoyed by the execution of Mary, Queen of Scots, a good Catholic.[1]

The Pope offered to pay $1,000,000 to Spain when the first English port was taken, thus appealing not only to the religious feelings of the Spanish but to their higher instincts, such as greed.

With their more maneuverable ships and heavier guns, the English riddled the Spanish fleet. Such Spanish galleons as were not sunk by gunfire were subsequently shattered by a storm. The English lost not a single ship and only twenty or so seamen killed. England was now mistress of the seas, and the way was open to colonialization of America. Had the English realized that this would lead to the Revolutionary War and the emergence of the United States, they might not have been so pleased with their victory.

There is always something that takes the pleasure out of winning.

[1] There was no real disagreement between the English and the Spanish on the execution of Mary, for the English themselves said, "A dead Catholic is a good Catholic."

CHAPTER XVI

The Thirty Years' War

THOUGH the Thirty Years' War must take second place to the Hundred Years' War as regards length, in one respect it is first. It is easily the most confusing.

It began as a religious war, a war of Catholics against Protestants. As was proved by the Crusades, when Christians fought Moslems instead of each other, it is not hard to persuade a person who really believes in his religion that anyone who believes in some other religion is his enemy or at least lacks an open mind. Devices used to open minds have included the sword, pike, halberd, arquebus, and musket. Persons with intense religious convictions make excellent soldiers.[1] They are sure that they will win, because God is on their side, or, if they lose, that they will go to Heaven—which, after years of freedom to loot and rape, is better than going home.[2]

[1] Unless, of course, they become conscientious objectors.
[2] A change, anyhow.

The wars of Protestants against Catholics actually began well before the Thirty Years' War. One historian says the conflict began in 1562, with the massacre of a congregation of French Calvinists, just sitting there enjoying a sermon about Hell and Damnation. This was ten years before the famous Massacre of St. Bartholomew, when more than ten thousand French Protestants, or Huguenots, were slain by Roman Catholics, though Saint Bartholomew emerged unscathed. It was obvious from this that Catholics and Protestants took their religion seriously and that there was ill feeling between the two groups.

An interesting military theoretician who influenced Cromwell, Gustavus Adolphus, and others was François de la Noue, called *Bras-de-Fer* because of an iron hook that replaced, somewhat unsatisfactorily, an amputated arm. Having fought in military campaigns for thirty years, this experienced Protestant soldier found time, while a prisoner of war, to write his *Discours Politiques et Militaires*. In this he advanced the theory that unrest in Europe was largely caused by the presence of idle soldiers who "felt it a social degradation to return to the plodding life of a farmer or tradesman." What soldiers hated to give up was the prospect of spoils, of which they would have none as farmers and only a little as tradesmen. La Noue wisely foresaw continual war as a way to happiness and a solution to the problem of unemployment.

Shortly before the start of the Thirty Years' War there were several colorful battles,[1] notably those between the Dutch and the Spanish. In one, the siege of Haarlem, the Spanish forces outside the city were suddenly surprised by a band of Dutch arquebusiers on skates.[2] We are told "they left several hundred Spanish dead on ice," no doubt preserving them for whatever nefarious purpose.

And then there was that extraordinary military episode in France, when the inhabitants of Villefranche decided to attack the neighboring town of Montpazier and loot it under cover of darkness. By coincidence, the inhabitants of Montpazier planned to do the same thing to Villefranche the very same night. Taking separate ways, the two parties did not meet, but each finding the walls of the other city undefended, pillaged and looted at will. It was ridiculously easy. According to the Duke of Sully, who relates this in his *Memoirs,* and might be making it all up, everyone was happy until each group returned to its own city and, by light of day, discovered what had happened. The whole incident points up the subtlety of assault, especially by night.

But these were all preliminaries to the Thirty Years' War, which began as a civil war between German Protestants and German Catholics but soon

[1] The prevalent color was a warm shade of red.
[2] Ice, not roller, but a surprise anyhow.

dragged in almost all the nations of Europe and involved other than religious motives. Wisely, however, these nations did most of their fighting in Germany, seeing no reason to mess up their own countries. As a result, after thirty years of being the battleground Germany lost half its population and was unable to recover for nearly two hundred years.[1]

The spark that set off the Thirty Years' War was when the Archbishop of Prague ordered a Protestant church destroyed and the Protestants retaliated by throwing a couple of Bohemian officials out a window. This was an old Bohemian way of indicating displeasure, popularly known as "defenestration." Unhappily for these officials, the window was not on the street level but on one of the upper floors.

Soon Spain, France, Denmark, Sweden, England, Italy, and other countries got into the fray. The religious issue became somewhat blurred when Catholic France and Protestant Sweden joined to oppose Ferdinand II, the Holy Roman Emperor and, according to his opponents, a holy terror. The only thing about the war that remained consistent was that it was a war of plunder.[2] The soldiers, being unpaid, depended on pillaging for food, and their leaders encouraged

[1] The wisdom of fighting wars in some other country has not been lost on the United States.

[2] Religious fervor helped, however. The Bishop of Würzburg put 9000 persons to death as witches and wizards in 1627–1628, a two-year high up to that time. That is more than were killed in many a battle, and the generals were envious.

them. At mealtime, instead of "Come and get it!" the cry was "Go and get it!" It is said that the soldiers of Tilly and Wallenstein, fighting for the Emperor Ferdinand, "devoured the countryside like a swarm of locusts." They had to keep on the move, forever shifting to a new place after picking the old one clean. Though they may not have been the greatest soldiers of all times, they were probably the hungriest.

As for Wallenstein, it must be noted that although a duke and a general, he also adopted the title of Admiral of the Baltic. It doubtless caused him no little chagrin when, suddenly having an opportunity to invade Denmark and strike a telling blow at the Protestants, he discovered he had no ships.

The great general of the Thirty Years' War turned out to be King Gustavus Adolphus of Sweden. Why Sweden, which in the twentieth century learned how much more convenient it is to remain neutral, got into the war is a matter on which historians disagree. The King, however, issued a call to fight "for house and home, for Fatherland and Faith," and these seemed worthwhile goals.[1]

Gustavus, sometimes called the Father of Modern War, developed mass killing into virtually an art. A humane leader, he did away with flogging. In the interest of discipline, however, in event of regimental misbehavior he ordered every tenth man, chosen by

[1] Many, too, admired his nice distinction between a house and a home.

lot, to be hanged.[1] Minor infractions of rules led to such appropriate punishments as loss of a hand, being shackled in irons, or running the gauntlet. But no flogging.

Gustavus honestly tried to protect his soldiers. Casualties (among his own men) distressed him. He encouraged his men to dig trenches, and thus may have been the originator of trench warfare. It is said that he himself often came onto the battlefield and wielded a shovel. When shots began to come close, he would dig at a speed that amazed his subordinates.

The changes in warfare and weaponry initiated by Gustavus were many. He developed regimental insignia—colorful silk ensigns embroidered with emblems and mottoes—which gave a man a sense of belonging and togetherness. The Army became a home away from home. He also instituted a staff system and increased the amount of paperwork. In this he was helped by Gutenberg, who made printing possible and paved the way for issuing orders in triplicate.

As for weapons, Gustavus shortened the pike from eighteen to eleven feet, probably by cutting seven feet off the handle. He also lightened armor, lightened the musket, and greatly improved the mobility of his forces. Instead of limiting cannon to use against fortifications, he massed them directly against enemy

---

[1] A chart showing the incidence of regimental misbehavior, after this law was published, indicates a substantial falling off.

soldiers, who thought there should be a law against this sort of thing. His field guns, displaying unusual versatility, fired both canister and grape, the latter, for greater destructiveness, retaining their seeds.

In 1632, after many successes, Gustavus "fell to an untimely death" [1] at the Battle of Lützen. He never had the satisfaction of knowing that his foe, General Albrecht Wenzel Eusebius von Wallenstein, was assassinated only two years later.[2]

Even without Gustavus and Wallenstein, the war went on, the thirty years still not being up. Improvements in weaponry also continued. The flintlock, which was to be used for the next 200 years, was invented about 1635. And the bayonet came into use at Ypres in 1647. In its first form, called the plug-bayonet, it was simply stuck into the muzzle of the musket, making firing more than a little difficult. But with the coming of the socket bayonet, which could be fastened to the side of the muzzle, infantry fighting was revolutionized, since foot soldiers could reload under cover of their bayonets. The pikeman and the arquebusier were now one. Or, as it has been more picturesquely stated: "The medieval and the modern

---

[1] Have you noticed how rarely anyone dies a timely death, in or out of war?

[2] For the tragic story of Wallenstein, see Schiller's *Wallenstein*. Schiller himself was an army surgeon who went AWOL to see a performance of one of his plays, and for this was put in prison. An interesting play, though never written, would have been Wallenstein's *Schiller*.

were wedded; the spear was now mated with the musket." Many a life was to be saved, and many a life was to be lost, by this ingenious combination.

Let us leave the Thirty Years' War on this optimistic note.[1]

---

[1] Germany having been so thoroughly devastated that it was no longer a suitable battleground, the Thirty Years' War ended in 1648 with the Peace of Westphalia. But with civil wars going on in England and France, there was never a dull moment.

CHAPTER XVII

Two Good Centuries

HAVING got off to a rousing start with the Thirty Years' War, the seventeenth and eighteenth centuries were, on the whole, good centuries for warfare. Consider, for instance, the advance made in England. As we have noted, religious wars began with the Crusades, between the Christians and Moslems. Then in the Thirty Years' War it was between Catholics and Protestants. In seventeenth century England there was further refinement, war being between two branches of Protestants. This seemed very nearly the ultimate.[1]

The Civil Wars in England were only partly religious. They were also between the Cavaliers and the Roundheads, the latter keeping their hair clipped

[1] In recent times, however, there is frequently a struggle within a single Protestant church, perhaps between those supporting the minister and those demanding his ouster. But these are not full-fledged wars, and indeed rarely result in bloodshed.

short and being considered peculiar by their opponents.[1] The Cavaliers, or Royalists, employed mostly
cavalry, while the Roundheads depended largely on
infantry. Stories that Roundheads were sometimes
used in cannon during a shortage of ammunition are
discounted by most historians.[2]

Oliver Cromwell, the leader of the Roundheads,
marched his troops up and down England. In one
battle he subdued the Scots. In another he subdued
the Irish. Once, walking over a battlefield strewn
with the bodies of 4000 dead, Cromwell was a little
subdued himself.

Cromwell was a tough general, and at the Battle of
Marston Moor, in 1644, gained the title of "Iron-
sides." Add to this an iron will, and it is easy to see
why he was almost invulnerable. Just to make sure,
however, he always said a prayer before going into
battle, something simple and devout, such as "Lord,
let me win." It seemed to work.[3]

Meanwhile, back on the Continent, things were
kept going by the Turks, who after twice trying to
take Vienna and being defeated, returned to Tur-

[1] Oddly, this is what is now thought of males who wear their
hair long.

[2] Charles I lost his head, but since he was a long-haired
Royalist, it could hardly have been mixed up with a pile of
cannonballs.

[3] Cromwell never lost a battle. Generals who are too busy
with reports and staff meetings to pray should keep this in
mind.

key. They decided they didn't want Vienna anyhow. Soon after, Russia became an important military power, at the Battle of Poltava defeating Sweden, which had been throwing its weight around the Baltic ever since the time of Gustavus Adolphus.

But the two nations that made a success of the seventeenth and eighteenth centuries militarily were France, under Louis XIV, and Prussia, under Frederick the Great.

Louis XIV believed in the divine right of kings. When a Frenchman swore, *"Mon Dieu!"* Louis smiled indulgently. *"L'état, c'est moi,"* he said, closely identifying himself not only with God but with the Government. Louis had the longest reign in Continental history, seventy-two years, and during most of that time managed to keep France at war.[1] His reason for making war on neighboring countries was completely rational and understandable. Instead of fighting for an idea or a religion, Louis fought for territory and profit. A Grand Monarch, with expensive habits such as Versailles and Madame de Maintenon, he took France to war with great singleness of purpose: to balance the budget.

One of the changes in warfare instituted by Louis XIV was establishment of the Quartermaster Corps. Louis wanted to make sure his men were well dressed

---

[1] Since he was only five years old when he became King, he had to content himself with playing with toy soldiers until he could assume actual command.

and well fed, as befits the soldiers of the Sun King.[1]
Instead of making them forage and pillage and take
food away from the poor peasants, Louis had them
supplied by the Quartermaster Corps, which took
food away from the poor peasants in a more civilized
way, by taxation.[2]

Under Louvois, his Minister of War, there were
other innovations. Infantry came to fight in a line, instead of a column, and to keep the line straight neces-
sitated hours and hours of drill. As we are told, "The
bark of commands rang out on every parade ground
of the realm." It must have been about this time that
drillmasters learned to bark, instead of speak. The
best-known drillmaster was Jean Martinet, whose
name is immortalized in the dictionary, along with
chauvinist and quisling. Under Martinet, infantrymen learned to advance at the cadence of eighty steps
a minute, to fire in a single volley at the word of command, and to fall to the ground immediately upon
being shot through the head.

Louvois greatly improved the morale of troops by
calling it *esprit de corps*. He also made generous use
of medals and ribbons for distinguished service, and
adorned his officers with epaulets, lace, plumes, and

[1] Before Louis XIV, according to one historian, "The French
shrank from service abroad." That shows how poorly they
were fed.

[2] The word, in those days, was "levy," but the effect was the
same.

embroidery. A wise Minister of War, he appealed to vanity, a human quality that had previously been overlooked.

The French at first jumped on Holland, thinking to put the squeeze on William of Orange. But though helped by England, after twenty-two months they gave up and signed a treaty. It is at about this point that historians begin to use the expression "The ink had scarcely dried on the treaty when. . . ." [1]

Mostly Louis picked off easy opponents, such as the Great Elector of Brandenburg, who had a big name but a small military force. But finally, after nibbling at first one little country and then another ("He confined himself to one mouthful at a time," one historian puts it), he turned everyone against him and had to fight most of Europe. In the years that followed, there were many famous victories and many famous defeats, from the battle of Blenheim to the Battle of Malplaquet. With the Peace of Utrecht, in 1714, "the aggressions of Louis XIV ended just fifty-one years after his first seizure."

Just before his last seizure, on his deathbed, the Grand Monarch made an interesting confession. "I have been too fond of war," he said. Before anyone could argue with him, he was dead.

---

[1] It was this same treaty that led one historian to remark, "William of Orange swallowed his rage for three days after the conclusion of peace." Every time he thought of it, later, it gave him a lump in the throat.

Passing over a succession of wars, such as the War of the Spanish Succession, the War of the Polish Succession, and the War of the Austrian Succession, and noting that the most significant improvement in infantry arms in two hundred years was the substitution of an iron for a wooden ramrod by Leopold of Anhalt Dessau in 1740, we come to Frederick the Great of Prussia, who by coincidence ascended the throne that very year.[1]

Under Frederick the Great, discipline was all-important. "The soldier must be made more afraid of his own officers than of the dangers to which he is exposed," he wrote, encouraging officers to arrogance, flogging, and, it must be confessed, unpopularity. Inducements to obtain recruits included low pay and kidnaping. The enlistment period was usually for life.[2] Innovations of Frederick the Great included the oblique attack, or approaching the enemy at an angle—which would have been completely new had it not been used by Epaminondas in the Battle of Leuctra in 371 B.C.; marching fire, which meant continuing to march ahead while reloading, and took guts;[3] and yelling during a cavalry attack "to increase the moral effect."[4]

[1] Was it a coincidence or was it something ordained by fate? Somehow it is hard to imagine Frederick the Great fooling around with a wooden ramrod.

[2] Which, fortunately, might not be long.

[3] Especially when hit in the stomach.

[4] What is moral about yelling at a man while you are killing him is not explained.

Frederick's cavalry was divided into three types: cuirassiers, dragoons, and hussars. The busiest were the hussars, whose assignment was to bring back men attempting to desert.

Like Louis XIV, Frederick began by taking small pieces of territory nearby, hoping nobody would notice. He started by taking Silesia, a part of Austria, two months after he came to the throne. With more than usual frankness (he was new at the business), he gave as his reasons for aggression "an army quite ready for action, the money all found, and perhaps the desire to make a name." After all, he had nothing to lose but the lives of a few thousand soldiers.[1]

But, like Louis, before long Frederick had everyone against him—not only Austria but Russia, France, Sweden, and Saxony. Frederick was upset. While others accused him of being an aggressor, he wrote hundreds of pathetic letters to people all over Europe. He even threatened suicide. There were those who thought this was a splendid idea. But many were softened up in what was an early instance of "going over the heads of leaders to the people." In fact not a few were convinced by Frederick's arguments that seizure of a neighbor's territory is a Good Thing.[2]

[1] Frederick himself, who had a practical streak (of yellow), fled from the battlefield, thinking he had lost when actually he had won. It was not a subject that guests brought up at the dinner table.

[2] A century later Thomas Carlyle, writing in a safe spot in London, considered Frederick admirable. Time heals all wounds except gunshot wounds through the head.

One authority goes as far as to say that "Frederick's talents as a propagandist served his country perhaps better than his generalship." However, Frederick did not depend entirely on propaganda. In the Battle of Leuthen, against the Austrians, he lost one man in five and yet won, a masterpiece of bloodshed praised by Napoleon.

Wars were getting shorter. After the Hundred Years' War and the Thirty Years' War, we have the Seven Years' War (1756–1763), which was basically a struggle over Silesia, which Frederick had taken from Austria, as we have noted above. There were numerous battles, in one of which, the Battle of Zorndorf, the Prussians suffered 38 per cent casualties and the Russians 50 per cent. It was probably this battle that inspired Voltaire to write in *Candide:* "The cannon first of all laid flat about six thousand men on each side; then the musketry removed from the best of worlds some nine or ten thousand blackguards who infested its surface." Certainly, in battle after battle, Frederick did his best to reduce the population of Europe, and his best was very good indeed.

At the end of the Seven Years' War, national boundaries were about the same as at the beginning. But lives had been well spent. Frederick retained Silesia.

In the latter part of the eighteenth century, warfare took an interesting turn. A war was fought in America instead of Europe, and over taxation instead of the desire to acquire territory.[1] Without going into all the details of the Revolutionary War, it can safely be said that the British soldiers, in the end, found scarlet coats more suitable for hunting foxes than being shot at; a new infantry technique was discovered when the colonists did not fire until they could see the whites of the Britishers' eyes;[2] and the colonists were fortunate in obtaining military instruction from men like Baron von Steuben and Thaddeus Kosciusko, who imported the fine points of killing from the Old Country.

By the close of the eighteenth century the cost of warfare was rising, due mainly to the increase in artillery. Arms factories were in great demand, and these in turn stimulated the growth of capitalism. The contribution of war to industrial progress, which would never have entered the minds of old warriors like Alaric and Charlemagne, was at last becoming evident. Henceforth, death and taxes were to become inseparable.

[1] At last a cause for war was discovered that had widespread popular support.

[2] Which, fortunately, were not too bloodshot, until afterward.

CHAPTER XVIII

Napoleon

FROM the time he was a small boy, Napoleon wanted to be a soldier. He entered military school at the age of ten, and could hardly wait to take command of an army and start slaughtering the enemy, whoever that might be. "He had a weak mouth," says his biographer, but that proved no impediment to a manly military career that included one stretch of almost twenty years of continuous war.

The name of Napoleon must be included in that roster of dedicated men, including Alexander, Hannibal, Caesar, Attila, Genghis Khan, and the inventor of gunpowder, who by their unceasing efforts spared millions of men from suffering the ills and boredom of old age.

Napoleon was born Napoleon Buonaparte, and it is perhaps significant that he took the *u* out of his name about the time of his first military campaign.[1]

[1] Some think he became more self-centered. However, though he took out *u* he did not put in *I*.

It is also significant that Corsica, where Napoleon was born, was ceded to France only a year before his birth, thus making him French rather than Italian (Genoese).[1] What is most intriguing about Napoleon's career, however, is that in 1782 he was recommended for the Navy by one of the inspectors of the school he was attending. But appointment of a new inspector the next year frustrated this plan, and the young man instead proceeded to the military school in Paris and specialized in artillery. It is interesting to contemplate a naval career for Napoleon, perhaps culminating in his being blown off the bridge by the guns of Lord Nelson.[2]

Napoleon was under average height, and it has been said that had he been two inches taller the fate of Europe might have been different. His being short gave him an urge to excel in other ways. It also caused him to sit on a horse as much as possible, so he could look down on people.[3] Though he is known as the Little Corporal, he advanced through the ranks with better than average speed, becoming a brigadier general when he was twenty-four and Emperor when he was thirty-five.

[1] France was thus led in its wars of conquest by a Frenchman, thereby escaping the embarrassing fate of Germany, led by that Austrian, Hitler.

[2] It would have been appropriate, after all, had Waterloo been a sea battle.

[3] Subsequent dictators have given up the horse in favor of the reviewing stand and the balcony.

Napoleon's mind was always on war and conquest. He was forever scheming, planning, trying to get ahead.[1] But his energy was not boundless, and he, too, sometimes grew tired. Evidence of this is to be found in his rather pathetic words: "When I see an empty throne, I feel the urge to sit down on it." Many tourists today, trudging from room to room through one of Napoleon's palaces, have the same urge, though any old chair would do.

The part played by Josephine in Napoleon's military career is unknown, but the fact that he left on his Italian campaign two days after he married this woman, six years his senior, may have some significance.

Napoleon early saw the close connection between the military and the political. During his Italian campaign he did himself no harm, as it turned out, by sending presents to the Directors, large sums of money to the nearly bankrupt treasury, and works of art (including a bust of Caesar) to the museums of Paris. Everyone was happy to be remembered, and so appropriately, when they might have had no more than an occasional picture post card with a description of the carnage of battle and a friendly "Wish you were here." To young officers wishing to get ahead, Napoleon could still be taken as a model.

[1] He once thought of a literary career. Entering an essay contest, his placed fifteenth out of the sixteen essays submitted. He knew, though, that if he became a great conqueror he would have no difficulty finding a publisher for his memoirs.

There were few changes in weaponry at this time, but Napoleon was greatly helped by universal conscription, adopted by the revolutionary government of France in 1739. The French Army was thereby increased to nearly 750,000, the largest group of people intent on killing since the days of the barbarian migrations. Also, scientific talent was mobilized, church bells were melted down to make cannon,[1] and cabinetmakers and metalworkers were drafted to manufacture muskets. Flour mills were transformed into producers of gunpowder.[2] Napoleon's personal surgeon, Larrey, was active on the battlefield, sometimes making as many as 200 amputations in a single day. He may not have whistled while he worked, but the shells did.[3] Everyone was happy at last to be doing something useful.

As for tactics, Napoleon believed in using great masses of artillery, bayonet charges, and hitting his opponents where they were weakest.[4] He also increased the cadence of his infantrymen from seventy

[1] This was done in most subsequent wars, making cities quiet enough to hear gunfire in the distance.

[2] "Let them eat gunpowder," said one Parisian cynic. The choice was not between guns and butter but between guns and bread, and the choice was clear.

[3] I know you don't believe that figure of 200 amputations in one day, and neither do I. But it is in Brig. Gen. William A. Mitchell's *Outlines of the World's Military History*, p. 352. Napoleon made Larrey a baron for his feat, and probably not only for his feat but for legs and arms.

[4] Often in the head.

paces a minute to a hundred and twenty. Having a great deal of territory to conquer, he could afford no dilly-dallying. As he galloped past his foot soldiers, the look he gave them seemed to say, "Is that as fast as you can walk?" [1]

Nonetheless, Napoleon's soldiers loved him. They admired the way he could wear a hat like that, and keep it on, the way he could ride at full gallop with only one hand on the reins, the other nonchalantly tucked into his tunic. He had style. He had class. He had charisma. At that time, moreover, he was winning. The morale of Napoleon's troops in the Italian campaign is indicated by the statement that, in one battle, "Hundreds of cheering grenadiers were shot down by grape or canister." They seemed to be enjoying it.

After Napoleon's success in Italy he undertook to invade Egypt, but despite his victory at the Battle of the Pyramids, he was forced to return to France when the British fleet cut off his source of supplies. Even then, the spirit of Napoleon was shown when one of the French ships, sunk by British guns, "went down with all hands shouting *'Vive la République!'*" [2]

In the years that followed, Napoleon fought a series

[1] "I may lose battles," Napoleon said, "but I do not lose minutes." No one ever had to cool his heels waiting for Napoleon, but some overheated them keeping up with him.

[2] Unfortunately, while their hands were shouting, their mouths were swallowing water. This is known as "the confusion of battle."

of campaigns against the Austrians, British, Prussians, Spanish, Russians, and anyone else who stood in his way. Except for the British naval victory at Trafalgar, when Nelson failed to see the order, "Leave off action," because he chanced to place his telescope to his blind eye,[1] and went on to destroy the French fleet, the French under Napoleon dashed from one triumph to another. Once, when a battle was going against him, Napoleon seized the French standard and (fortunately wearing boots) walked over a pile of bloody corpses and rallied his men to victory.

However, Napoleon did not fare so well in his invasion of Russia. Though he overwhelmed the Russians at Borodino and entered Moscow, the Russians "burned Moscow over his head," [2] leaving him no winter quarters for his troops. He was forced to retreat through the snow and ice. The bad weather, the bad roads, and the bad Cossacks combined to ruin his army. Thousands of his soldiers were frozen to death. Not more than 100,000 (some say 50,000) of his original force of 550,000 (some say 450,000) came out of Russia. Even Napoleon was a little cold [3] and discouraged. The only Frenchman to profit from the whole enterprise was Jean Meissonier, the artist, whose painting of Napoleon leading his troops back

---

[1] There was only a 50 per cent chance of his doing this.

[2] Another indication of Napoleon's unfortunate lack of height.

[3] Except for that right hand, tucked snugly inside his coat.

through the snow to Paris was a highly successful depiction of defeat.

After the retreat from Moscow, it was all downhill for Napoleon. This does not mean it was easy. It was hard. Out of his exile to Elba came, of course, the famous palindrome, "Able was I ere I saw Elba," one of the longest sentences to make sense whether read forward or backward. Then there was the escape from Elba, followed by the Hundred Days, the Battle of Waterloo, and Napoleon's final years on St. Helena, brooding, writing his memoirs, and asking himself "What went wrong?"

However many lives may have been lost, but for Napoleon we would never have had the Code Napoleon, the Napoleonic Era, the napoleon (*1.* a French gold coin worth twenty francs, *2.* a form of pastry consisting of oblong layers of puff paste with a cream filling) , or Napoleon's Tomb. His place in military history is secure.

CHAPTER XIX

Wars in America

FOR A TIME, after the Battle of Waterloo, things looked bad for war in Europe. People resigned themselves to a long period of dull, unexciting peace. But the invention of detonating powder by a Scottish clergyman, Alexander Forsyth, who had been trying to find a way of arousing his slumbering congregation, led to the percussion-firing weapon, which in turn made possible Samuel Colt's revolving pistol in 1835. The .44 Colt revolver, the long bullet (replacing the round missile), and the American rifle played a large part in Winning the West. This was the great period of killing Indians, Bad Guys, and persons slow on the draw, and it had a lasting impact on the motion-picture industry.

War and weaponry, lagging in Europe, found a new home in America. Even before Waterloo, war broke out between the United States and England when the British not only searched American vessels on the high seas, but impressed American seamen, many of whom screamed, as they were carried bodily onto British ships, "I am not impressed!"

At the beginning of the War of 1812, as at the beginning of most of its wars, the United States was unprepared. The regular army numbered 6744 men. But during the war, by means of volunteers and militia, the total was raised to 527,000, against a British invading force of 53,000.[1] It was an interesting war tactically, a war fought for the freedom of the seas which began with an invasion of Canada and ended with General Andrew Jackson's victory at New Orleans fifteen days after the treaty of peace was signed. As a matter of fact, two days before war was declared the British Government had stated that it would repeal the laws that were the chief excuse for fighting. But at the beginning of the war, as well as at the end, the word didn't get through. One historian has called the War of 1812, which was mostly fought in 1813, 1814, and 1815, "The War of Faulty Communication."

But if the treaty that ended the war made no reference to what had supposedly started the hostilities, and if no issues were settled, there were nonetheless important gains for the United States. The war in-

[1] It has always been an American principle that you should outnumber your enemy, and odds of ten to one would appear to be adequate. At sea, however, the British had nearly a thousand fighting ships as against only seventeen frigates and sloops of the U.S. Navy. This, obviously, was unfair.

spired Francis Scott Key to write "The Star-Spangled Banner," [1] and it led to the election of two of its heroes, Andrew Jackson and William Henry Harrison, to the Presidency. It also stimulated the United States to build a new Capitol and White House, the old buildings having been burned down by the British after the Battle of Bladensburg. For a war that lasted only two and a half years, these were better-than-average accomplishments.[2]

By 1846, the United States was down to an army of 5300 men and obviously in that traditional state of unpreparedness, mentioned above, that signaled the beginning of a new war. This was the Mexican War, fought over the southwestern boundary of Texas. Should it be the Nueces River or the Rio Grande? Added factors were the Manifest Destiny of the United States to expand westward and the weakness of the Mexican government. Moreover, the United States offered to pay Mexico $25,000,000 for New Mexico and California, and there was a chance that Mexico might decline this generous offer. War seemed the obvious solution.

American troops, pushing into Mexico, won a series of successes under General Zachary Taylor and

[1] An inspirational anthem, even though the average citizen is unable to reach the high notes.

[2] Nor let us forget that at the Battle of New Orleans the Americans killed 2100 British in twenty-five minutes. This is almost one hundred a minute, a record that was to stand for some years.

Major General Winfield Scott.[1] By the time the Americans entered Mexico City, Mexico was willing to sell New Mexico and California for $15,000,000, a clear saving of $10,000,000 over the original price, with Nevada, Utah, most of Arizona, and parts of Colorado and Wyoming thrown in. If one of the purposes of war is to gain territory, the Mexican War is an excellent example, the United States having acquired more than 525,000 square miles. Also, according to custom, one of the heroes of the war, General Zachary Taylor, subsequently became President of the United States (see Jackson and Harrison, above). And useful training for the next war was given to officers like Ulysses S. Grant, William T. Sherman, George B. McClellan, Thomas "Stonewall" Jackson, and Robert E. Lee.

All in all, the Mexican War was a richly rewarding experience.

Save for the publication of Karl von Clausewitz' *Vom Kriege,* in 1832, and the Crimean War, in 1854, Europe was still lagging militarily. There had not been a really good battle since Waterloo. As for Clausewitz, in his classic work he developed the "annihilation principle" and "the bloody solution of the crisis," and has been hailed as having fathered "the most bloody and wasteful era of warfare in modern

[1] General Taylor, a man of commendable foresight, won several battles before the war officially began.

times." Unhappily, he died a year before publication
of his book, and was not around to enjoy its success or
to observe the application of his theories.

The Crimean War, which came about when
France, Turkey, and Great Britain joined forces to
keep Russia from pushing through Turkey to get an
outlet to the Mediterranean, was a confusing affair
and did the cause of war no good. When the allies
landed in the Crimea, someone had forgotten the
maps, and officers found it embarrassing to ask the
Russians if they were on the right road. Someone also
blundered at the Battle of Balaclava, as Tennyson
pointed out in "The Charge of the Light Brigade."
But the Crimean War produced Florence Nightin-
gale. Henceforth nurses gave ill and maimed soldiers
something to look forward to during hospitalization.[1]

But despite the Crimean War and the writings of
Clausewitz, Europe was decadent militarily, with only
such minor efforts as the Seven Weeks' War between
Prussia and Austria, until 1870.[2] We must turn again
to America for a war of respectable proportions.

The Civil War, which began in 1861, proved that
men had not lost the knack of killing on a large scale

[1] Some, during the Victorian period, feared for the safety
of nurses among all those men. But with a hypo in one hand
and a bedpan in the other, they proved well able to take care
of themselves, if they wanted to.

[2] Consider the decline from the Hundred Years' War, and
even the Seven Years' War, to the Seven Weeks' War. People
began to ask themselves, "What has gone wrong?"

and over a long period. Instead of only seven weeks, it lasted four years. Instead of only a few thousand, around 525,000 men were killed, which established a new record. Though civil war goes back to the Greeks and cannot be claimed as an American invention, this one was fought on a new geographic principle, between the North and the South.[1]

The tide of battle flowed first this way and that, in battles like Antietam, Bull Run, Chancellorsville, Chickamauga, Gettsyburg, Shiloh, and Vicksburg. The soldiers of the South were led by General Robert E. Lee, who was well-dressed and gentlemanly. The soldiers of the North were led by General Ulysses S. Grant, who despite his sloppy appearance became President of the United States (Lee, not to be outdone, became President of Washington College, later Washington and Lee University) and made half a million dollars out of the sale of his memoirs. Many think Lee was a greater general, but they grudgingly admit that Grant won.

Without going into the details of the Civil War, such as Pickett's Charge, which was modeled on the Charge of the Light Brigade and was a similarly brilliant exercise in mass suicide, mention should be made of advances in weaponry. One of these was the use of armor on ships called ironclads. After the *Merrimac* and the *Monitor* had pounded and rammed

---

[1] What some feel is now needed is a war between the East and the West.

each other for three hours without serious damage, a British admiral was quoted as saying, "The man who goes into action in a wooden ship is a fool, and the man who sends him there is a villain." Wooden ships henceforth were Out.

More important, during the Civil War the magazine-loading rifle and the machine gun were invented, and torpedoes, land mines, the field telegraph, breech-loading weapons, rifled cannon, wire entanglements, hand grenades, flame throwers, booby traps, armored trains, submarines, torpedo boats, and balloons were tried out. Despite the great von Moltke's description of the Civil War as a war in which "two armed mobs chased each other around the country," it was actually a war that, in addition to freeing the slaves and making Lincoln's Gettysburg Address possible, contributed greatly to warfare for the next century. The few hundred thousand men lost did not give their lives in vain.[1]

Brief mention should also be made of the Spanish-American War, the last war America was involved in during what had been an exciting nineteenth century. Since the author of a book of 752 pages says "The causes which led to the outbreak of the Spanish-

[1] Contradicting von Moltke, Bernard and Fawn Brodie, in *From Crossbow to H-Bomb,* p. 133, call the American Civil War "a colossal proving ground for improved weapons of all kinds." Sometimes, carried away by sentimentality concerning Grant's drinking habits, Lee's surrender, and the devastation of the South, we forget these solid gains.

American War are too numerous and too involved to
be discussed in this text," I shall not try to explain
them either. Suffice it to say that, with the regular
army down to 28,183 men, conditions once again
were ripe for war. After the sinking of the battleship
Maine in Havana Harbor, the United States took
quick evasive action by invading the Philippines.
Also Theodore Roosevelt ran up San Juan Hill, and
later ran for President. With very little loss of life,
the United States won Cuba, the Philippines, Guam,
and Puerto Rico. But, being a little embarrassed to
have got off so cheaply, it paid Spain $20,000,000.

Thus it was that America shouldered the load and
kept up the tradition of war while Europe, exhausted
from the Napoleonic struggle, gained strength to go
at it again.

CHAPTER XX

The Franco-Prussian War

THOUGH there are more complicated explanations, including France's desire to keep the Hohenzollern family off the throne of Spain,[1] the real reason for the Franco-Prussian War was Bismarck's policy of blood and iron. Instead of worrying about iron-poor blood, Bismarck thought there was too much blood-poor iron, in the form of unused bayonets and shells. As Bismarck knew, Germany was prepared for war and France was not. Besides, Napoleon III[2] had a kidney ailment that made it hard for him to sit on a horse, and it was therefore difficult for him to provide leadership.[3]

By means of short-term enlistments, which provided a large army reserve, Prussia and her German

[1] The French thought Hohenzollern a ridiculous name for a Spanish king.

[2] A third-rate Napoleon.

[3] He could get onto a horse, but he was always having to get off.

allies were able to raise 1,180,000 men within two weeks after the opening of hostilities. An extra inducement was the Iron Cross, a handsome medal that not only looked nice but if the wearer were lucky might deflect a bullet. With the Iron Cross went extra pay. What better incentive to enlist?

The French were defeated at one battle after another, and at Sedan made a cavalry charge against the German infantry comparable to the Charge of the Light Brigade and Pickett's Charge, noted above, that almost succeeded. It almost succeeded, that is, in outdoing either of its predecessors for heroic slaughter. One historian has admiringly called it "a gallant exhibition of waste of life." It would take years of reproduction to replace the young men lost, but the French, undaunted, could hardly wait for the end of the war to plunge into the task.

Meanwhile, back on the battlefield. . . .

Though the French used the mitrailleuse, a form of machine gun with as many as thirty barrels that could be fired either simultaneously or successively, they were unsuccessful. The mitrailleuse had been kept such a secret, for fear the Germans would learn about it, that soldiers were not trained in its use. Just before a battle, they would be handed a package which, when opened, contained an odd-looking weapon. When they looked puzzled, an officer with Top Secret clearance would tell them, "That's a mitrailleuse. Go ahead and use it." The mitrailleuse was the first of a long line of secret weapons, some so secret that they were never heard of.[1]

Much of the Franco-Prussian War was an effort between the two forces to take the offensive. Sometimes the French were more offensive than the Germans. Sometimes the Germans were more offensive than the French. The French, using the bayonet, often attacked with cold steel, hoping to warm it up in German blood. The Germans, on the other hand, "chewed up the French with their artillery," a crunching, munching sound that could be heard for miles.

At Sedan, it is said, Napoleon III tried to be killed in action, knowing he had not long to live and wishing to be remembered as a hero. Unfortunately, however, he was captured and had to live three years longer.

With the victory of the Germans over the French at Sedan, the war might well have ended. But though the Regular Army had collapsed, the French people, as it has been said, "flew to arms." This was almost as spectacular as the flight of the French leader, Léon

---

[1] The mitrailleuse, it should be added, fired not only old iron and grapeshot but coins. In the heat of battle it was pathetic when a soldier ran out of ammunition and had nothing on him but paper bills. "Can you change a twenty?" he would ask his buddy, hoping he could get enough centimes to keep firing at the advancing Germans.

Gambetta, who escaped from encircled Paris by balloon to rally the countryside.[1]

The Germans were vexed by *francs-tireurs*, free-shooters who did not operate in accordance with rules laid down by the German General Staff. But the Germans set an invaluable precedent in dealing with these unorthodox fighters. They "shot the nearest mayor," [2] burned villages and farms, and otherwise indicated their disapproval.

Nonetheless, the French held out in Paris for 131 days, their rations finally getting down to horsemeat, rats, and wine. When the wine gave out, they surrendered. It had been a long siege, made possible only by the indomitable spirit of the French and their genius with cuisine. They at last ran up the white flag, though some think it was a napkin.

The most important contribution of the Franco-Prussian War was the discovery of the profit motive. As General Mitchell points out in his *Outlines of the World's Military History*, pp. 544–46, the Germans received not only an indemnity of one billion dollars from the French, the largest indemnity ever paid up to that time, but much else of monetary value. To put it in tabular form:

---

[1] Gambetta has been described as "a fiery orator," and one can imagine his filling his balloon with hot air, while the people of Paris stood around and cheered.

[2] Who, after all, was easier to hit than one at a distance.

EXPENDITURE BY THE GERMANS

War expenses	$500,000,000
Men lost (40,000 @$700)	$28,000,000
Total	$528,000,000

RECEIVED FROM THE FRENCH

Indemnity	$1,000,000,000
Alsace and Lorraine (4700 square miles, at current land value)	$212,000,000
Inhabitants of Alsace and Lorraine (1,500,000 persons @ $350, or half the value of a German soldier)	$525,000,000
Total	$1,737,000,000

NET GAIN TO GERMANY	$1,209,000,000

Add to this the moral profit—which, as General Mitchell says, "was worth much more to the nation and its individuals in prestige, self-reliance, and power," and it is evident that this was a more than adequate profit for six months' work.

Even the loser gained. The French economy was so stimulated by the war that the indemnity of

$1,000,000,000 was paid in less than three years.[1]

As this great conflict proved, war is not only exciting, a way to keep your mind off your troubles, but it
pays.

[1] *The World Book Encyclopedia,* Vol. 6, p. 2746. I am dedicated to this work not only for such facts but for learning
about the francolin, a type of partridge I might never have
known about had this entry not followed directly after that
about the Franco-Prussian War. Once I start reading, I find
it hard to stop.

CHAPTER XXI

World War I

GERMANY having discovered that aggression pays and that, in von Moltke's words, "in war man's noblest qualities are developed," it was only a question of time until that nation would have a go at it again. Other countries, faced with this prospect, began to fortify their frontiers. "Good fences make good neighbors," they said nervously.

Leaving the French and others at work with their cement, barbed wire, and gun emplacements, let us look briefly at a few wars that filled in the time until 1914.

One was the Russo-Turkish war in 1877. The cause of the war was simple and understandable. The Russians, who had been wanting to take Constantinople for hundreds of years, thought that at last the time was ripe.[1] But despite their defeat of the Turks at the

[1] Some of the Turkish officers were overripe. There were lieutenants fifty years old, and one lieutenant colonel was ninety-three. Promotion was slow.

siege of Plevna, they once again stopped short of Constantinople. If the Russians were disappointed, they did not show it. They had been fighting the Turks, off and on, since 1569, and there would be another opportunity. Had they taken Constantinople, there might have been a spiritual letdown. It is good to have a goal, something yet to achieve.

Another war was the Boer War in 1899, in which the British put down rebellious Dutch settlers, known as Boers,[1] in South Africa. Using a long-range rifle with smokeless powder, the Boers, who had developed considerable skill in hunting wild animals, at first picked off the British at long range. Even after the British had won, overwhelming the 75,000 Boers with a force of 450,000 men, small bands of the defeated enemy took to the hills and for two years continued to bring down an occasional Britisher, along with other game.[2]

Finally, though we can hardly wait to get to World War I, we must make brief mention of the Russo-Japanese War of 1904–1905. The cause of this war was the uncontrollable desire of both Russia and Japan to control the Far East, especially Korea. The Japanese, a little impatient, attacked the Russians two days before war was declared. Though Russia was a much larger country than Japan, and should have

[1] Pronounced either "boor" or "bore," and in neither case very flattering.

[2] Hunters on safari are now limited to fauna indigenous to the veldt.

won, it was defeated at Mukden and Port Arthur. One military historian gives as the reason the fact that the Russian soldiers were much larger than the Japanese, and therefore better targets. This does not explain, however, the victory of the Japanese Navy under Admiral Togo.[1] At any rate, Japan emerged as a first-rate power and could take pride in being called "The Prussia of the Orient."

And now, at last, we come to World War I, which until World War II was known simply as the World War.

World War I had everything one could ask of a war: not much of a cause, inconclusive results, and enormous cost in lives and property damage.[2] In many ways it was a perfect war, and it was widely believed that there would never be another, because how could it be improved upon?

The war began in 1914, when the Austrian archduke was assassinated at Sarajevo by a Serb.[3] Thanks to a series of alliances, Austria-Hungary declared war on Serbia, then Germany on Russia, then Germany on France, then Great Britain on Germany, then

[1] According to one source, the Russian ships had "foul bottoms," and it is probably just as well they were sunk.

[2] Almost eight million soldiers were killed, along with some two hundred billion dollars in cost to the participating nations. War had, indeed, come a long way since the feeble efforts of Genghis Khan.

[3] Some think the Kaiser contributed to the start of the war. For several years he had been going around rattling his sword, and this made everyone nervous.

Austria-Hungary on Russia, then Serbia on Germany, then Montenegro on Austria-Hungary, then France on Austria-Hungary, then Great Britain on Austria-Hungary, then Montenegro on Germany, then Japan on Germany, then Austria-Hungary on Japan, then Austria-Hungary on Belgium, then Russia on Turkey, then France on Turkey, then Great Britain on Turkey, then Italy on Austria-Hungary, then San Marino on Austria-Hungary, then Italy on Turkey, then Russia on Bulgaria, then Bulgaria on Serbia, then Great Britain on Bulgaria, then France on Bulgaria, then Italy on Bulgaria, then Germany on Portugal, then Austria-Hungary on Portugal, then Italy on Germany, then Rumania on Austria, then Germany on Rumania, then Turkey on Rumania, then Bulgaria on Rumania, then the United States on Germany, then Panama on Germany, then Cuba on Germany, then Greece on Germany, then Siam on Germany (now Germany was really beginning to get it), then Liberia on Germany, then China on Germany, then Brazil on Germany, then the United States on Austria-Hungary, and finally Panama on Austria-Hungary. It got so that when the leader of a country was overheard to exclaim, "I declare!" the nation was at war.

Though the Western Front is best known, there were also Eastern, Italian, and Balkan fronts, providing a total of 2195 miles of battle lines. As one historian says, "These battle lines were long enough to stretch from Chicago to San Francisco," but fortunately they never did. With enemy forces facing each other for such a great distance, there was a constant demand for manpower, and young men had almost unlimited opportunity to advance.[1]

A new kind of warfare developed along these battle lines. This was trench warfare, which permitted soldiers to live for months in the relative safety [2] and comfort of deep ditches which were partially filled with mud, lice, and pictures from home. Between the trenches of the opposing forces was an area known as No Man's Land, which no one entered unless he was very brave or had been commanded to and was more afraid of his commanding officer than of the enemy. Each side fought hard to keep from giving ground, not wishing to do all that digging again.

Poison gas, first used by the Germans in 1915 in the Ypres sector, brought an interesting new weapon into warfare. Poison gases included diphosgene, chloropicrin, hydrocyanic acid, and mustard gas. Some produced tears, others affected the central nervous system, and still others caused burns on the skin and respiratory tract. No one could accuse the chemists of shirking their responsibility in time of war. Defense against poison gas was provided by the gas mask, a

[1] Until mowed down by enemy fire. The British at one point took 45 square miles in five months at a cost of 370,000 men, or about 8200 casualties per square mile. As enemy resistance stiffened, so did bodies of the dead.

[2] I.e., safety from relatives.

great boon to the homely soldier who when wearing one looked as handsome as anybody. The only alternative to wearing a gas mask during an attack was holding your breath.

It was also in World War I that the tank made its first appearance. Its appearance was terrifying. Improbable as it seems, "The first tank was mounted on caterpillar tracks." The tracks of a caterpillar are none too easy to see, and early tank crews must have had excellent eyesight. The tank got its name from the British, who first developed it. It is said that in order to keep the real purpose of the machines a secret, the British gave out the story that they were tanks used for carrying water. When the Germans first came up against them, therefore, in the Battle of the Somme in 1916, they did not expect to be fired upon, or at any rate by anything more than water pistols, and were surprised and hurt.[1]

Like the tank, the submarine and the airplane were for the first time employed in this war. With its submarines, the Germans tried to stop the shipping of American supplies to the Allies in Europe, but the United States built merchant ships faster than the Germans could sink them. What with building ships and one thing and another, the United States spent $35,413,000,000 during World War I, but by such means as Liberty Loans, increased taxes, and raising

[1] It is hard to believe that the British would stoop to such duplicity, but I have this from an authoritative source.

the postage for a letter from two cents to three the money was found. As a result, Americans became convinced that money can always be found for a worthy cause, such as a war to make the world safe for democracy.

Germany finally agreed to an armistice on November 11, 1918. The Treaty of Versailles, on June 28, 1919, was signed in the Hall of Mirrors so that the representative of each country could see what was going on behind his back.[1]

Rarely has a war accomplished so much as World War I. It rearranged the boundaries of Europe to everyone's dissatisfaction, established the League of Nations,[2] imposed on Germany reparations of $33,000,000,000,[3] and, in the United States, made possible the American Legion and the Gold Star Mothers.

[1] Though President Wilson played a large part in drawing up the treaty, the United States never ratified it, preferring to make a separate treaty with Germany in 1921. Some thought this was not cricket, and they were right. It was politics.

[2] Which the United States did not join. See the preceding footnote.

[3] Which were not collected.

CHAPTER XXII

World War II

THOSE who considered World War I the ultimate in wars were lacking in vision, as was proved by World War II, which was of worldwide scope and truly worthy of its name. As one historian says, "It was fought on every continent and every ocean." With bombings of cities, it was a Total War in which even the humblest civilian could feel a sense of participation.

To prepare for World War II, Japan invaded China and Italy invaded Ethiopia. By so doing, they proved that wars of aggression could be carried on, just as they had been for hundreds of years, despite the League of Nations. The Spanish Civil War may have cost the lives of a million Spaniards, but was well worth it as a way of testing new types of weapons.

Hitler, the German leader, had an old-fashioned idea, which was, simply, to conquer the world. But he went at it in an imaginative new way. For one thing, he explained his plans in *Mein Kampf,* instead of keeping them a secret as conquerors had always done before.[1] For another, he made a treaty of friendship with a country, to show his good will, shortly before invading it. Or sometimes, as with Austria, instead of signing a formal treaty he simply gave his word of honor. In this instance he did not march across the border until he had stated firmly, "Germany has neither the wish nor the intention to annex or unite with Austria." He dealt with Czechoslovakia in still a different way. After taking the Sudeten border area, he said this was his "last demand," then waited a full six months before seizing the rest of the country. Everyone was impressed by Hitler's reasonableness, as well as by his large, superbly trained military force.

World War II officially began on September 1, 1939, when Hitler's troops invaded Poland at dawn. Hitler had been invading countries for several years without causing hard feelings, but this time—perhaps because he attacked at such an ungodly hour—Great Britain and France declared war. Others joined the Allies, until there were forty-one countries, from Argentina to Yugoslavia, ranged against what came to be called the Axis.[2] One of those somewhat late in

[1] What people couldn't understand was that, though the approach was novel, the book was nonfiction.

[2] An axis is defined as "a straight line, real or imaginary,

coming to the assistance of Germany was Italy, which entered the conflict when the French were in retreat and it looked as if the war was about over. In all fairness, it must be said that Italy made a great contribution by invading the French Riviera, and at the height of the tourist season.[1]

An innovation in World War II was the *Blitzkrieg,* or lightning war, which enabled the Germans to conquer all of Poland in less than four weeks. Ground and air, infantry and tanks, were coordinated. Hitler agreed with Macbeth that "if it were done when 'tis done, then 'twere well it were done quickly." But Hitler also participated in the *Sitzkrieg,* when for seven months the Germans sat in the Siegfried Line and the French in the Maginot Line. Seldom have so many sat on so much for so long. It was a poor way to fight a war if you are going to roll up a decent toll of casualties.

In general, however, Hitler contributed greatly to the progress of warfare. Ingeniously, he sent troops to Norway in ore boats. When the soldiers popped out, they laughingly told the Norwegians they were oresmen. He went around the Maginot Line and attacked it from the rear, which was something the French ob-

---

passing through a body." What passed through bodies in World War II was usually real—a bullet, a bayonet, or a piece of shrapnel.

[1] Later, when the Italians were having trouble taking anything, Hitler took Greece and gave it to them. *"Das ist für Sie,"* said Hitler. *"Grazie,"* said Mussolini.

viously had not counted on. He invaded the Low-lands without declaring war, thus increasing the element of surprise. And he overran Luxembourg in a single day, his task made somewhat easier by the fact that Luxembourg had no army.[1]

World War II saw the introduction of underground warfare, barrage balloons, Selective Service, searchlights, tracer bullets, radar, bazookas, parachute forces, WACs, over-age destroyers,[2] Lend-Lease, car pools, and saturation bombing. This last was a technique whereby a great many bombs were dropped, usually at night, in the hope that some would hit the target. It may have been terrifying to civilians in the vicinity, but it greatly improved the morale of munitions makers.

The Germans used dive bombers,[3] while the Allies developed long-range heavy bombers. The heaviest raid by the *Luftwaffe* was on Coventry, when 200 tons of bombs were dropped. But before the war was over, the Allies had dropped 363 times as many bombs on Berlin. Manpower was increasingly in demand not only to manufacture bombs and to drop

[1] Another reason he overran Luxembourg was that the country was so small. After overrunning it, the Germans checked their maps and came back more slowly.

[2] Not soldiers but ships, fifty of which were given by the United States to Great Britain as a reminder of the long friendship between these two countries.

[3] So called because the British, when they heard them coming, cried out, "Dive! Bombers!"

them from planes but to keep track of the number and tonnage.

The first intimation that Hitler was human [1] came with his defeat at Stalingrad. After signing a non-aggression pact with Russia (which should have been the tip-off), Hitler invaded that country. But the Russian "scorched-earth" policy [2] and, especially, their removal of factories just before Hitler got to them, proved frustrating. Hitler began to see parallels between himself and Napoleon other than the fact that they were both, at one point, corporals.

Japan, having learned the *Blitzkrieg* (which they called *Britzklieg*) technique from Germany, attacked the United States at Pearl Harbor. They did so without declaring war or, indeed, saying a word about it. [3] The United States then came into the war on the side of the Allies, and not a year too soon. Soon after, with Americans landing in Africa and Sicily and stepping on the toe of Italy, [4] things went from worse to better, or alphabetically from D-Day to V-Day, culminating in the unconditional surrender of Germany and later,

[1] Some still refuse to believe this.

[2] Things weren't merely scorched, they were burned to a crisp.

[3] A technique also learned from the Germans.

[4] At which point Italy, realizing it had been wrong about a German victory, became a "co-belligerent" with the Allies. If this was not exactly changing sides, it was becoming belligerent in another way. Mussolini hung around for a while, but he was soon at the end of his rope.

after two atomic bombs had been dropped, of Japan.[1]

Hitler, though no golfer, committed suicide in a bunker. The Japanese Emperor, Hirohito, after agonizing soul-searching,[2] decided he was not divine, after all, and left that sort of thing to General MacArthur.

The war ended, after six fruitful years, with a host of new records. In the armies of the Allies and the Axis, something over 14,000,000 men were killed. No one knows precisely how many civilian casualties there were, and the carelessness of accounting is indicated by the fact that the figure varies from 12,000,000 to 25,000,000. Ironically, for those interested in statistics, Japanese civilian casualty figures were destroyed in an air raid.

But even without knowing the exact number of persons killed and mutilated, this was undoubtedly the biggest war yet. Whether it was also the best is a moot point, depending on whether you are primarily interested in quantity or quality.

---

[1] In the interest of space, or *Lebensraum,* it will be noted that a few of the events of World War II have been treated somewhat briefly or, still better, omitted entirely.

[2] He never found it.

CHAPTER XXIII

World War II$\frac{1}{2}$

DEVELOPMENT in war and weaponry after World
War II, and prospects for wars that will keep
pace with the progress of civilization, can be summa-
rized briefly.

In accordance with a custom of long standing, maps
were redrawn after World War II.[1] Also according to
custom, maps were redrawn in such a way as to provide the maximum excuse for future conflict. A
stroke of genius was the dividing of the former capital
of Germany into East and West Berlin and placing
West Berlin in an area surrounded by East Germany.

Since nationalism is always helpful in generating
wars, numerous new nations were created. The first
aim of these so-called emerging nations was to de-

[1] If munitions makers profit during a war, mapmakers
profit during the months immediately following a war. The
importance of war to publishers, commercial artists, and the
manufacturers of paper and ink should not be underestimated.

velop an army and to obtain weapons from one of the larger, more cultured nations, until it could raise its educational level to the point where it could manufacture its own.

The atomic bomb, used against Japan at the end of World War II, was called "the deadliest invention since gunpowder." But it was soon overshadowed by the hydrogen or thermonuclear bomb, and the most spectacular wedding since the ceremony uniting Prince Rainier and Grace Kelly was that which has been described as "the marriage of nuclear warheads to missiles capable of ranges up to five and six thousand miles and of fantastic accuracy at those ranges." [1]

The frequently mentioned nuclear club is not, as one might think, a throwback to the Stone Age—a stick which, when one is beaten over the head with it, will cause a low-yield thermonuclear explosion. Actually, the Nuclear Club is an exclusive organization founded by the United States and later joined by Russia, France, China, and other nations, all of which were uninvited. Members of the club pay no dues and, in fact, very little attention to the wishes of any other country.

Since it takes two to make a war, and since the most effective results, in terms of casualties and devastation, are achieved when the two countries have approximately equal power, the outlook was bleak when only the United States had the hydrogen bomb,

[1] The marriage vow was climaxed by "till death us do."

which it successfully tested in November 1952. But the Soviet Union exploded a similar bomb less than a year later, and everyone breathed more easily.[1] Other countries quickly got onto the bangwagon.

In the years since its discovery, ways have been found to make the hydrogen bomb more rapidly and more cheaply. As a result, such bombs are no longer in short supply.[2] In fact, the only problem is likely to be storage space, and a war may become necessary in order to use up some of the old bombs and make room for newer models. Fortunately, hydrogen bombs can now be made smaller and lighter. This should not only help solve the storage problem but eventually make it possible for everyone to carry a thermonuclear bomb in his pocket, instead of a pistol. Going into battle, a soldier would have such a bomb hanging from his belt in place of a hand grenade. The possibilities of destroying both one's enemy and oneself are exciting indeed.

Even during this period of waiting for World War III we have not been without activity and advance. Though war is no longer called war but "police action," "peace-keeping," "rebellion," or "putting down rebellion," something resembling what was once known as war continues from time to time in

[1] Though perhaps not so deeply, because of the fear of inhaling nuclear fallout.

[2] One expert, hoping to encourage those who have become concerned about food shortages, refers to "nuclear plenty."

such widespread parts of the world as Latin America, the Middle East, Africa, and Asia.[1]

An interesting new development is modified war, in which war is modified by an adjective, thus giving us cold war, hot war, just war, unjust war, clean war, dirty war, guerrilla war, and limited war.[2] All of these wars except the cold war are fought with what are called conventional weapons. The cold war [3] is fought with unconventional weapons, such as radio, television, newspapers, spies and/or diplomats, intelligence, counterintelligence, and lack of intelligence. Meanwhile the stockpiles of thermonuclear bombs, or the Real Thing, are growing, and more and more nations are joining the Nuclear Club. There are now sufficient bombs to kill everyone on earth not only once but several times, provided people cooperate and keep coming back to life.[4]

[1] Fastidiously avoiding use of the term *war,* a military spokesman refers to "the application of military force to obtain an objective." According to *Webster's New International Dictionary,* Second Edition, a "solemn war" is one that is begun by a formal declaration. There is more spontaneity and gaiety about the other kind.

[2] Etymologically examined, "guerrilla" means "a little war." From this we get the poetic line, "A little warfare is a dangerous thing," as well as the similarity of a little war and a little pregnant.

[3] Also known as a war of nerves. Have you ever seen one nerve fighting another, or felt as if it were?

[4] This is known as overkill, or making sure.

In short, prospects have never been brighter.[1]

To conclude this history of war and weaponry, which it is hoped will be widely read not only in this country but also in the Soviet Union and China, I quote this recent statement by an eminent biologist: "Insects, better fitted to survive, could take over the world after a nuclear war." The following lines, though revealing a certain softness regarding the human race and ill becoming an objective historian, are nonetheless included to fill out these final pages:

> Just think how ants
> Would prance
> And preen,
> A merry scene
> For ants, at least;
> How they would feast
> Nor need to heed
> The poison paste
> Adroitly placed;
> How flies would fly,
> No swatter nigh,
> And gaily zoom
> From room to room;

[1] The thermonuclear bomb, with its fusion of hydrogen atoms, is said to approximate in a small way conditions prevailing on the sun. Should such a bomb be dropped close to you, it would be a wise precaution to look at it through a piece of smoked glass.

How bugs, quite free
From DDT,
Would nibble flowers
For hours and hours. . . .
But, insects all
Who crawl
Or hum,
Who'd drop the crumb?
Who'd plant the garden?
I beg your pardon,
Bugs. I insist
That we'd be missed.

BIBLIOGRAPHY

THOUGH it would seem unnecessary, anyone wishing to read further on this subject might glance at such works as:

R. G. Albion, *Introduction to Military History*, 1929

Johann von Bloch, *Der Krieg*, 6 vols., 1899

Bernard and Fawn Brodie, *From Crossbow to H-Bomb*, 1962

Neville Brown, *Nuclear Warfare*, 1965

H. S. Cowper, *The Art of Attack*, 1906

Maurice R. Davie, *The Evolution of War*, 1929

Hans Delbrück, *Geschichte der Kriegskunst*, 1900

J. F. C. Fuller, *Armament and History*, 1945

J. F. C. Fuller, *A Military History of the Western World*, 3 vols., 1955

B. H. Liddell Hart, *The Decisive Wars of History*, 1924

Henry W. L. Hime, *The Origin of Artillery*, 1915

William A. Mitchell, *Outlines of the World's Military History*, 1931

Lynn Montross, *War through the Ages*, 1944

John U. Nef, *War and Human Progress*, 1950

Charles Oman, *A History of the Art of War,* 1898

Sir Ralph Payne-Galleway, *The Projectile-Throwing Engines of the Ancients,* 1907

Theodore Ropp, *War in the Modern World,* 1959

Fernand Schneider, *Histoire des Doctrines Militaires,* 1957

Edwin Tunis, *Weapons, a Pictorial History,* 1954

W. W. Tarn, *Hellenistic Military and Naval Developments,* 1930

A. W. Wilson, *The Story of the Gun,* 1944

Quincy Wright, *A Study of War,* 1942

As a sample of the delightful reading to be found in some of these works, I quote from Cowper's *The Art of Attack,* p. 274, where he is discussing the trebuchet, a twelfth-century improvement on the ancient catapult:

These siege engines throw other missiles besides stones and javelins. They throw millstones, flaming projectiles, putrid corpses, and live men. A dead horse in the last stage of decomposition bundled up and shot by a trebuchet into a town of which the defenders were half dead with starvation, started a pestilence. . . . Manure and offal, and even the bodies of dead soldiers, were used in the same way. William of Malmesbury describes the Turks at Antioch throwing from their petraries (catapults) the heads of townsmen into the Frankish camp. . . . An envoy or messenger was sometimes tied up alive and cast back into the town.

If this fascinates you, be sure to read in Payne-Galleway's *Projectile-Throwing Engines,* p. 39, about the siege of Carolstein, in 1422, when "Coribut caused the bodies of his soldiers whom the besieged had killed to be thrown into the town in addition to 2000 cartloads of manure. A great number of the defenders fell victim to the fever which resulted from the stench."

When you have finally read enough and are ready to play, I suggest Joseph Morschauser's *How to Play War Games in Miniature,* 1962. Using toy soldiers, guns, and tanks, and playing with chance cards or dice (the singular of dice is die), you can either replay the great battles of history or make up some of your own. After playing an exciting war game with realistic soldiers made in Germany, you may find it a little hard to go back to model trains.

$\mathcal{A} \, \mathcal{B} \, O \, U \, T \quad \mathcal{T} \, H \, \mathcal{E} \quad \mathcal{A} \, U \, \mathcal{T} \, H \, O \, \mathcal{R}$

Richard Armour says he is "an occasional and selective militarist," and in the present book feels "like a sinner writing against sin." It may be helpful to know that the author of this work of blood and irony served in the Army in both World War II and the Korean War, rose to the rank of colonel, and was twice decorated with the Legion of Merit. Though firm in his conviction that war is wicked and senseless, he thinks it indicative of the imperfection of the human race, and therefore likely to be with us for a long while. Yet, the eternal optimist, he has hope for man.

Richard Armour's search for facts has led him to a lifetime of scholarship that has included a B.A. from Pomona College, a Ph.D. from Harvard, research fellowships in England and France, and professorships at such institutions as the University of Texas, Northwestern University, Wells College, the University of Freiburg, the University of Hawaii, the Claremont Graduate School, and Scripps College, where he was also Dean of the Faculty. He has lectured or been guest-in-residence on over two hundred campuses and has lectured abroad as an American Specialist for the State Department.

His search for absurdity has produced a long string of

best-selling books, from *It All Started with Columbus* to *Twisted Tales from Shakespeare,* and from *The Classics Reclassified* to *Going Around in Academic Circles,* as well as thousands of pieces of verse and prose in the leading magazines of the United States and England. Now emeritus (which he says means "out of merit"), he concentrates on writing and lecturing. His home, when he is home, is in Claremont, California. Equally faithful to his wife and his typewriter, he has been married thirty-five years and has written thirty-five books.